"Don't you really love me?"

by Rev. Joseph M. Champlin

AVE MARIA PRESS
Notre Dame, Indiana 46556

Dedication

"As a consequence, with the help of advances in psychology and in the art and science of teaching, children and young people should be assisted in the harmonious development of their physical, moral and intellectual endowments. Surmounting hardships with a gallant and steady heart, they should be helped to acquire gradually a more mature sense of responsibility toward ennobling their own lives through constant effort, and toward pursuing authentic freedom. As they advance in years, they should be given positive and prudent sexual education" (*Declaration on Christian Education* of the Second Vatican Council, para. 1).[1]

This book is dedicated to two men by the name of John. The first one was a Pope of courage and vision who saw the need for modernization of the Catholic Church and summoned his fellow bishops to Rome to begin the task. The second John, equally courageous and visionary, was a President who set noble ideals for every American and then passed the torch to the new generation for whom this book is directly written. May it share in the spirit of those two great leaders and in their vast impact upon modern man.

NIHIL OBSTAT:
> John L. Reedy, C.S.C.
> *Censor Deputatus*

IMPRIMATUR:
> ✠ Most Rev. Leo A. Pursley, D.D.
> *Bishop of Fort Wayne-South Bend*

Contents

FOREWORD BY MAX LEVIN, M.D. 4

INTRODUCTION 6

1. LOVE IS A MANY-SPLENDORED THING 10

2. MEN AND WOMEN ARE DIFFERENT.
   OR ARE THEY? 30

3. PICKING YOUR PARTNER 55

4. LOVE AND LIFE 77

5. WHY WAIT UNTIL MARRIAGE? 98

6. HOW FAR CAN WE GO? 123

7. THE NEW GENERATION
   SPEAKS OUT 144

8. STARTING OVER 154

9. CHARTING THE COURSE AHEAD 173

EPILOGUE 195

ACKNOWLEDGMENTS 200

NOTES 202

BIBLIOGRAPHY 206

Foreword

Father Champlin's book is a powerful statement in support of the Judeo-Christian code in the field of sex. His argument is based on psychological rather than theological grounds. The book is not a collection of sermons. Instead, it is an exercise in pastoral psychology.

The priest, the minister and the rabbi all labor under a handicap today. In many circles morality is a dirty word, and the teachings of the clergy are met with skepticism if not disdain. But moral codes represent the felt needs of a society and should be viewed in terms of those needs. A moral code may have been handed down to us in theological language, but even an atheist, who rejects theology, ought to go behind the language and consider the code in terms of the social needs for which it was designed.

There is a clear example in the Talmud. The Talmud records that the ancient rabbis held a debate on the question, "What must have motivated the Lord to deliver the Israelites from bondage in Egypt?" What decision did the rabbis reach? If you and I were to guess the answer, we might suppose that the rabbis, as men of religion, arrived at an answer based on theological doctrine; for example, the Israelites refused to bow down before Egyptian idols. But no, the rabbis concluded that the Lord decided to deliver the Israelites *because they did not go to prostitutes*. This conclusion, an affirmation of marital fidelity, has a profound sociological meaning.

The delivery of the Israelites from bondage was a cultural advance, a step forward in the evolution of their society. In order to advance, a society must be made up of mature men and women who produce successive crops of healthy children. The growth of a society is facilitated by marital fidelity and retarded by infidelity. Children develop best in a family where father and mother are devoted to each other and to them. Children need the love and attention of their parents. A father who chases after women can't be a good father. Instead of giving time and thought to his children, his mind is elsewhere. He is wondering what alibi he can cook up for the weekend trip he wants to take with the blonde he met at the cocktail lounge. And so, in a society where infidelity prevails, children will be deprived. But in a society that puts a premium on sound family life, children have a decent chance to develop emotionally. This is a constructive conception, that sound family life strengthens the children and thereby promotes the society that they will take over from their parents. The ancient rabbis have given us a sharp insight into the sociological wisdom of the Judeo-Christian code. Far from being an arbitrary edict handed down by autocratic authority, the code can stand on its own inherent psychological sense.

Our young people today are confused, and their parents are too. They yearn to be sophisticated. We must help them to appreciate the instinctive sociological wisdom that guided our forefathers. Perhaps they will then begin to understand that morality is more than an autocratic dictate, that the Judeo-Christian code serves a constructive sociological purpose and is worth preserving as a guideline even today. True sophistication implies an appreciation of the realities of life.

I was about to say that Father Champlin's book ought to be required reading in our high schools and colleges. But today the word "required" tends to elicit the rejoinder, *Who's gonna make me?* Perhaps, then, it would be better to say that the book should be recommended reading for our students and young adults, be they Catholic, Protestant, Jewish—or atheist.

Max Levin, M. D.

Dr. Levin, a psychiatrist, is clinical professor of neurology at the New York Medical College in New York City and visiting neurologist, Flower and Fifth Avenue Hospitals, Metropolitan Hospital Center in New York.

Introduction

In the opening pages of Jacqueline Susann's dreary, but very popular, *Valley of the Dolls*, the reader meets Neely, an exuberant, gurgling 17-year-old who has toured in vaudeville since she was a young girl. Neely's friend and across-the-hall neighbor is Anne Welles, a prim, proper and frigid New Englander. Anne is a refugee in New York, seeking to escape the dull stiffness of her home town and the strict puritanism of her family background. She hopes to discover warmth and life in the big city.

But those harsh, restrictive views on love and sex follow her. One day Anne criticizes her friend for a comment she has made approving casual sex. Neely, exasperated at such apparent naiveté about these matters, explodes:

> "Anne, you not only talk like a virgin but you think like a priest. Look, I'm a virgin, but I do know that sex and love are two different things for a man . . . . I've hung on to my virginity because I know men put a high value on it, and I want some man to love me the way Charlie loves Kitty. But it's different with a man. You don't expect *him* to be a virgin."[1]

I doubt if Neely would pick up this book. In her view, virgins and priests just don't seem to understand sex and love. And I am a priest. A Roman Catholic priest, celibate, unmarried and childless.

Even if Neely did read this book, I am not sure she would agree with it. She accepts, or at least reflects in this conversation, the double standard of morality. For her, men and women follow different rules. Women are expected to be virgins; men are not. I do not subscribe to that double moral code of sexuality.

I feel that men and women must assume equal, even

if different, responsibilities during the dating, courtship, engagement period.

Let's consider the hypothetical but typical case of a couple named Tony Wood and Ann Phillips.

Tony and Ann have been dating steadily for several months. In his car on the way home from a Saturday-night date, Ann sits in the middle of the front seat, content and close to her friend.

As they near a public parking area on the shore of Lake Delta, Tony asks, "Shall we stop for a while?"

Ann nods and he noses the car into an open spot.

They talk. For a long while and about many things—war, peace, school, work, each other, their future. A romantic atmosphere surrounds them—the night is quiet, city lights reflect on the lake, the moon is full.

Tony takes Ann into his arms, holds her, kisses her, embraces her. She responds.

Soon she senses Tony is getting aroused. Ann pushes gently away, slightly breathless herself, feeling a break might help the situation. A frustrated frown creeps over Tony's face. With a partly hurt, partly irritated tone of voice, he pleads, "Don't you really love me? I mean, we love each other, don't we?"

His question splits her heart in two. Yes, she does love Tony, or at least she's very fond of him. And she does so much enjoy being close to him and would like to give in to some heavy petting, even perhaps go all the way. But something stops her . . . something tells her not to let herself go, something says that this may not be the best way to keep alive the wonderful relationship that has started between them.

The dilemma confuses Ann. She is not quite sure of the answer herself. How then can she possibly explain all of these feelings to Tony, now, in the car, under this pressure, without hurting him?

Tony, in turn, is wondering. Deep down he senses a voice warning him to hold back, telling him to think of the consequences, asking him to consider how Ann will feel later. But the voice is quite feeble and his feelings are so strong. He *is* frustrated. An emotional tidal wave wants to drown out that voice, sweep away all reserve and silence every one of Ann's objections.

This book is, directly, for the real couples in our contemporary society, persons largely in their teens and twenties, for whom this problem is not a theoretical puzzle posed in the classroom, but an unresolved, anxious question that arises frequently in their lives. It is for *both* the young woman *and* the young man. I hope this book will help the girl solve the dilemma, give the correct answer and understand what is involved if she is, consciously or otherwise, leading the boy to a position where he will ask the question. I hope it will also help the boy recognize his heavy responsibility in such situations, help him realize that it is unfair deliberately to place a girl in the dilemma Ann faces, unwise to take advantage of her now in a weak moment and ask her to do something she will regret later, unjust to expect her to be solely responsible for the decision on how far to go.

This book is, indirectly, for the parents of these young couples. Present-day communication in matters of sex between parent and children on the elementary school level is bad enough; communication in these delicate areas on the high school and college levels is even worse. I would like to think that my frank treatment of the subject in this book may possibly promote discussion of it by the family within the home. That still remains the ideal, the most suitable place for sex education.

ACKNOWLEDGMENTS

This book sprang out of a dozen years' experience dealing with couples in love. The thoughts it expresses came either from young men and women or from books or articles about them. For this reason I thank several groups of young Americans with whom I have worked: the juniors at Cathedral Academy in Syracuse, the seniors at Central Technical High School, the freshman and senior student nurses at St. Joseph's School of Nursing, and the 200 members of my class in the Summer School of the Christian Apostolate at Syracuse in July, 1966, as well as other college and high school students in the Eastern section of the United States who heard me and whose encouragement and enthusiasm spurred me to putting the thoughts in print.

I also thank the many individuals and couples who sought assistance from me either inside or outside the confessional. These frequently perplexed people found both support and solace in the ideas contained here.

Some of my material is original, but much has been taken from a variety of other sources. The frank quotations from contemporary fiction may disturb a few readers. But the references, while realistic, are not, I think, overly disturbing. Acknowledgment, as far as possible, is made in the text and in the bibliography to books or articles which supplied insights. But many contributors for whose assistance I am grateful have slipped into oblivion.

No man is an island. Nor does any author ever write a book alone. I cannot name all who lent assistance but I would like to acknowledge several who made major contributions: Dr. Max Levin for his Foreword and the following for their professional help and advice: Mr. Kenneth Peters, my editor at Ave Maria Press; Mrs. Muriel Ketchum of the English faculty at Central Technical High School in Syracuse; Rev. Charles E. Curran, a moral theologian currently teaching at the Catholic University of America in Washington, D.C.; Rev. John E. Corrigan, a parish priest in the archdiocese of Washington whose writings on confession and the sacrament of Penance have gained national recognition; Dr. Richard H. Aubry, assistant professor, Department of Obstetrics and Gynecology, State University of New York, Upstate Medical Center, and his wife, Mary, both of whom carefully read the manuscript and offered suggestions based on his technical background and their family life. Finally, my gratitude to Miss Veronica Kearney for her faultless typing of the manuscript and to Mrs. Virginia Walsh and Mrs. Nancy Barry for their aid in the clerical work required to obtain necessary copyright permissions. Needless to say, I alone still must accept the responsibility for any fault or weakness the book may contain.

1.   *Love Is a Many-*

$\mathcal{T}$he return of Leslie Rawlins Kind to normal health seemed probable, but uncertain. The probability offered her husband, Michael, some hope; the uncertainty of it all brought him constant anguish. Michael Kind was 45 and paunchy and the father of a son, Max, 16, and of a daughter, Rachel, 8. He was also a Reform rabbi currently serving Temple Beth Sholom in Woodborough, Massachusetts.

His wife's extended confinement in a local hospital imposed obvious burdens upon him and upon the two children. There was a lonely, empty house, heavy concern for the children, always wearing and sometimes discouraging work with his congregation, unceasing anxiety about Leslie . . . . Michael's pensive face reflected the worry and strain.

During a free afternoon on a late December day the rabbi was spreading fertilizer over the garden behind their New England home. His son came on the scene and pitched in with a second shovel. After working together for some time Michael asked him:

"Speaking of kisses, want the car New Year's?"

"I don't think so. Thank you." Max threw a last shovelful and straightened up with a sigh.

"How come?"

"I don't have a date. Dess and I aren't going steady any more."

He looked for signs of scar tissue.

"She was asked out by this older guy. He's already going to Tufts." He shrugged. "That was that." He knocked manure from the shovel blades. "The funny thing is, I'm not even upset. I always figured I was ape over her. That if anything ever broke us up, I'd be real shook."

"You're not?"

"I don't think so. The thing is, I'm not even seventeen, this thing with Dess was like . . . well, a dry run. But later, when you're older, how do you tell?"

"What's your question, Max?"

"What's *love*, Dad? How do you know when you really love a girl?"

He saw it was a serious question, one that troubled the boy. "I don't have a workable definition," he said. "When the time comes, when you're older and you meet a woman you want to spend the rest of your life with, you won't have to ask" (From Noah Gordon's best-selling novel, *The Rabbi*).[1]

The Michael Kinds, with their loves and their lives, will be back from time to time in this book. But the rabbi does help us right now to get started on what love really is. He did not have a workable definition. But that is hardly a surprise. Nobody seems to have one. Priest-psychiatrist-author Ignace Lepp in his *The Psychology of Loving* explains the reason why:

> "Since everybody talks about love and everyone actually experiences love to some extent, it might be thought that no notion could be clearer and more precise than the notion of love. The truth, however, is just the opposite. Like every other profoundly existential reality, love can barely be defined."[2]

Because love can barely be defined, we use the word in many ways and with an endless variety of meanings. In one 24-hour period a high school girl could easily say the following things: "I love God, I love my father, I love my mother, I love my brother, I love my sister, I love my boyfriend, I love pizza, I love myself." And it would be an impossible task to determine exactly what she means each time she employs the word "love."

Even good old Charlie Brown and Peanuts add little definiteness: "Love is walking hand in hand. Love is mussing up someone's hair. Love is having a special song. Love is tickling. Love is a valentine with lace all around the edges. Love is wishing you had nerve enough to go over and talk with that little girl with the red hair. Love is letting him win even though you know you could slaughter him. Love is hating to say good-bye. Love is a letter on pink stationery. Love is wondering what he's doing right now this very moment. Love is not nagging. Love is a phone call. Love is committing yourself in writing. Love is being happy just knowing that she's happy . . . but that isn't so easy."[3]

Charles M. Schulz, the creator of *Peanuts*, has captured many warm love experiences in this book, *Love Is Walking Hand in Hand*. He has added some insights. He has broadened our vision. But a workable definition, he has not offered us.

This chapter will not do much more than that either. I plan, by way of examples, to arrive at a certain basic notion of love and then to describe four elements necessary for that kind of love. I hope it will help clear away some false notions. I hope also that the boy who asks or the girl who responds to the question "Don't You Really Love Me?" will, as a result, understand better what true love should mean.

Selfish or Self-giving

1. A happy, teen-age student, mouth stuffed with food, exclaims, "I love pizza."

2. A middle-aged man has noticed his expanding middle and his receding hairline. He would like to deny, but must admit, that he is not as handsome as he was in his twenties, that he is on the downward slope of life. Nor is his wife as slim and attractive and affectionate as she was in those first years of marriage. In a moment of weakness he suggests a dinner date to one of the pretty, young unattached things bouncing around the office. She accepts. The evening moves on. Wine brings warmth and a sense of the old days. There is no really deep feeling for his companion. But later, parked, to satisfy her pleas for reassurance and to encourage her response, he halfheartedly whispers, "I love you."

3. An engaged couple on the West Coast are returning home from their evening together. They begin

to cross a large boulevard. Midway, he spots a car, rapidly, crazily, bearing down on them. He shouts. She panics. Frightened, frozen to the spot, she screams. He pushes her to the curb. She is safe, but he is not. A thud, a roar, terrible stillness, horror, sobbing, crowd, sirens, police, men in white, broken bones, lifeless body. The man's death speaks eloquently, "I love you."

4. Damien the Leper wrote the following about his work on Molokai:

"Leprosy, as far as is known, is incurable; it seems to begin by a corruption of the blood. Discolored patches appear on the skin, especially on the cheeks; and the parts affected lose their feeling. After a time this discoloration covers the entire body; then ulcers begin to open, chiefly at the extremities. The flesh is eaten away, and gives out a fetid odour; even the breath of the leper becomes so foul that the air around is poisoned with it. I have had great difficulty in getting accustomed to such an atmosphere. One day, at a Sunday Mass, I found myself so stifled that I thought I must leave the altar to breathe a little of the outer air, but I restrained myself, thinking of our Lord when he commanded them to open the grave of Lazarus, notwithstanding Mary's words, 'by this time there will be an odor.' Now my sense of smell does not cause me so much inconvenience. I enter the huts of the lepers without difficulty. Sometimes, indeed, I feel no repugnance when I hear the confessions of those near their end, whose wounds are full of maggots. Often, also, I scarcely know how to administer Extreme Unction, when both hands and feet are nothing but raw wounds."[4]

Damien left his European home and familiar faces for a strange island and unknown people. Their bodies were an ugly sight, but they were still persons. They could commit sin and need forgiveness, grow discouraged and need support, fear death and need hope.

When Damien de Veuster first sailed from Europe his body was healthy; when he made the final return, in a coffin, it was rotted with the same leprosy that had

claimed so many on Molokai. The legend is famous—
the priest one day proclaimed in a sermon at Mass,
"We lepers," announcing to his flock and to the world
that he also was now one of them, a leper. Damien's
life silently spoke to the lepers: "I love you."

The meaning of these examples should not be pushed
farther than intended, particularly the second and third.
The hypothetical case of the businessman and the actual
instance of the engaged couple involve enormously
complex situations. Brevity of description necessarily
produces an oversimplification. I use the illustrations
merely as starting points for discussion and as a means
to arrive at a possible root meaning of love.

The first two situations contain a common element.
The love professed is fundamentally self-centered,
selfish. The teen-ager loves pizza simply for what it
does for him. It tastes good, it satisfies his appetite.
Once the pizza no longer fulfills that function and can
be of no use to him, the love vanishes. The teen-ager,
overstuffed with a dozen pieces, probably would cry out
a little less enthusiastically, "I love pizza." His love is
not directed to the pizza in itself, but simply to the
pizza insofar as it does something to or for him. He
uses the pizza.

The businessman, in the situation as briefly described, does not love the office girl simply for what
she is, as a person. His "love" is a selfish, self-centered
thing. Considered quite coarsely, she gives him some
emotional, physical pleasure and satisfaction. Viewed
more deeply, she bolsters his ego, makes him feel young
and important and potent again. But in all these ways,
she is only performing a function, serving his needs.
He is using her in much the same way that the teen-
ager uses the pizza. And once the function has been
fulfilled and the need satisfied, it is probable the "love"
similarly will vanish. He gets up and walks away,
leaving the girl possibly crushed, but at least wondering if she simply has been used.

The third and fourth cases also contain a common
element. The love professed is fundamentally self-
giving, unselfish. A young man who gives his life or
health for his fiancée hardly is using her. He receives
little, if anything, in return. He loves her as a person,

not as a thing. He sees value in her very being, distinct from any service or function she can perform, apart from any need of his that she could fulfill. As I said, we should not extend this illustration too far. Many people would act as heroically for a relative, a fellow citizen, an innocent child. Nor does such heroism necessarily prove the presence of that love between a man and a woman required for a successful marriage. But the love is fundamentally unselfish and self-giving.

It seems obvious that Damien's life was one of self-giving, tremendously unselfish love. Again, we should not go to an extreme and feel that there were no compensations for this kind of dedication. The leper priest, like every man, needed to love and be loved, to feel wanted. He surely found emotional and religious satisfactions in his efforts. But the point I make is that basically his love looked upon the lepers as persons. He did not use them. He simply sought what was best for them. He judged they had value as human beings without consideration for any service they could give him in return.

I think now we can establish a general, basic idea of true love. True love is fundamentally giving. More accurately, it is self-giving. Erich Fromm, the world-famous psychoanalyst, in *The Art of Loving,* supports this notion. "In the most general way, the active character of love can be described by stating that love is primarily *giving,* not receiving."[5]

That is a rather simple concept of love. But what it actually means for an individual is not so simple. For one it is giving blood to the Red Cross; for another, money to the United Fund. For a parent it may denote giving free time to school activities; for a teacher, giving energy to the day's class presentation. For a student love may entail giving one's ear to a troubled classmate who wants to talk (on the telephone, naturally) about a personal problem. Love may demand giving one's heart in sympathy to a friend saddened by death. The soldier may see love as giving his life for a cause he believes to be true. Possibly the most difficult type of giving is the receiving-giving—letting someone wait on you, quietly allowing a person to give to you, knowing that their giving brings them personal joy and happiness. Older, handicapped persons often find this a real hardship and resent well-intentioned helpers. Strong-willed and independent people also find this receiving-giving frequently irksome. They would prefer to struggle or work things out alone; it takes sensitive, self-giving love to perceive that the greatest love in a particular situation may be *not* to do something.

The uncomplicated description of love as self-giving may seem vague and elusive, but actually it is nothing of the kind. It is most challenging and personal. Who can say what love will demand today? The individual upon arising in the morning hardly knows all the developments which will face him during the day. He may anticipate a few major items, but even in those he cannot visualize all the circumstances and relationships involved. Thus, what love requires can be determined only by the individual himself and, often, only at the precise moment in which he encounters the issue at hand.

Fromm notes this complexity. "What is giving? Simple as the answer to this question seems to be, it is actually full of ambiguities and complexities."[6] From my list of illustrations, it may appear that this giving kind of love always entails "giving-up," sacrificing, being deprived of something, discharging a painful obligation. True enough, giving frequently does demand pain or self-denial of sorts (it is hard to listen to a long-winded, but troubled friend when there are a million and one things you must do that morning). But there is a return: a sense of being needed and wanted, a feeling of self-fulfillment and accomplishment, joy and contentment. The person who loves invariably experiences one or all of these reactions. Fromm explains this phenomenon in technical terms:

> "For the productive character, giving has an entirely different meaning. Giving is the highest expression of potency. In the very act of giving, I experience my strength, my wealth, my power. This experience of heightened vitality and potency fills me with joy. I experience myself as overflowing, spending, alive, hence as joyous.

Giving is more joyous than receiving, not because it is a deprivation, but because in the act of giving lies the expression of my aliveness."[7]

It seems to me that one of the marvelous fruits of present-day research has been the harmony discovered between the commands of God in the Old Testament, the teachings of Jesus Christ, the personal experience of men and the principles of psychology.

We usually link love as a command with Christianity and characterize the Old Testament as a religion of precepts heavily founded on fear. As a point of fact, however, the commitment to love our fellowman appears in the early books of the Bible. Leviticus 19:17 states: ". . . but you shall love your neighbor as yourself; I am the Lord."[8] Centuries later, Jesus was asked this question:

> "Teacher, which is the great commandment in the law?" And he said to them, "You shall love the Lord your God with all your heart, and with all your soul, and with all your mind. This is the great and the first commandment. And a second is like it. You shall love your neighbor as yourself. On these two commandments depend all the law and the prophets" (Matt. 22:34-40).[9]

The daily experience of men and the testimony of religious leaders and counselors confirm that the individual who truly loves other people often radiates happiness. It is a strange paradox that the more we are concerned about making other persons happy, the happier we become ourselves. The self-centered, wrapped-up-in-himself type many times is sad, troubled, constantly seeking some answer to his own misery. The solution frequently rests in his lack of love, the absence of concern for others.

Psychologists seek an explanation for this fact. Their conclusions verify that what God commands for men is actually what will bring man his greatest happiness. Erich Fromm comments, "The awareness of human separation—without reunion by love—is the source of shame. It is at the same time the source of guilt and anxiety. The deepest need of man, then, is the need to overcome his separateness, to leave the prison of his aloneness."[10] This, as he later develops, is accomplished by love.

Elements of Love

I hope that I have established the notion that love fundamentally entails giving, self-giving. Our understanding of love, however, should deepen if we consider four basic elements common to all types of love.

The first element is *care or concern* for the other person. We love someone and that love prompts in us an active concern for the life and growth of this individual. It should be noted that such love and care can in a correct sense be directed to our own selves as well as to other people. In addition, I think we should realize that concern for a person's life and growth may touch all aspects of his being, i.e., both the material and the spiritual. Damien loved the lepers of Molokai. However, his love was not limited to, nor even primarily directed toward, their bodily welfare. His faith saw beyond that and found something more both in them and in his labors for them.

These points can be made clearer through two examples, one illustrating in a positive way the presence of care and the second demonstrating, in a negative manner, the absence of it.

Truman Capote's superbly written *In Cold Blood* re-creates the brutal slaying of the Clutter family in Holcomb, Kansas. Perry Smith was one of the murderers—a strange and forlorn individual, an emotional question mark, the product of a broken and turbulent home. The reader develops a certain amount of pity for him as his character unfolds in the story. But few felt much compassion for him during his trial. He was alone, without friends. Except for a couple of people like Don Cullivan and Joe James.

Fairly soon after his capture and imprisonment, Smith received a letter from Reading, Massachusetts. Don Cullivan had known Perry briefly in the Army, heard of his plight and wrote a note offering friendship and help. The two corresponded and Don later was asked to come for the trial. Capote tells the rest:

"Many observers of the trial scene were baffled by the visitor from Boston, Donald Cullivan. They could not quite understand why this staid young Catholic, a successful engineer who had taken his degree at Harvard, a husband and the father of three children, should choose to befriend an uneducated, homicidal half-breed whom he knew but slightly and had not seen for nine years. Cullivan himself said, 'My wife doesn't understand it either. Coming out here was something I couldn't afford to do—it meant using a week of my vacation, and money we really need for other things. On the other hand, it was something I couldn't afford not to do. Perry's lawyer wrote to me asking if I would be a character witness; the moment I read the letter I knew I had to do it. Because I'd offered this man my friendship. And because—well, I believe in the life everlasting. All souls can be saved for God.'

"The salvation of a soul, namely Perry Smith's, was an enterprise the deeply Catholic undersheriff and his wife were eager to assist— although Mrs. Meier had been rebuffed by Perry when she had suggested a consultation with Father Goubeaux, a local priest. (Perry said, 'Priests and nuns have had their chance with me. I'm still wearing the scars to prove it.') And so, during the weekend recess, the Meiers invited Cullivan to eat Sunday dinner with the prisoner in his cell."

The murderer and his visitor-friend exchanged greetings and enjoyed the huge dinner Mrs. Meier had prepared. Perry talked a bit about thievery, about the murder, about his own feelings. The well-intentioned Cullivan probed for contrition and remorse on Smith's part. He found little, if any.

"Cullivan was silent, and his silence upset Perry, who seemed to interpret it as implying disapproval. 'Hell, Don, don't make me act the hypocrite with *you*. Throw a load of bull—how sorry I am, how all I want to do now is crawl on my knees and pray. That stuff don't ring with me. I can't accept overnight what I've always denied. The truth is, you've done more for me than any what you call God ever has. Or ever will. By writing to me, by signing yourself "friend." When I had no friends. Except Joe James.' Joe James, he explained to Cullivan, was a young Indian logger with whom he had once lived in a forest near Bellingham, Washington. 'That's a long way from Garden City. A good two thousand miles. I sent word to Joe about the trouble I'm in. Joe's a poor guy, he's got seven kids to feed, but he promised to come here if he had to walk. He hasn't showed up yet, and maybe he won't, only I think he will. Joe always liked me. Do you, Don?'

" 'Yes, I like you.' "

"Cullivan's softly emphatic answer pleased and rather flustered Perry. He smiled and said, 'Then you must be some kind of a nut.' Suddenly rising he crossed the cell and picked up a broom. 'I don't know why I should die among strangers. Let a bunch of prairiebillys stand around and watch me strangle. Shit. I ought to kill myself first.' He lifted the broom and pressed the bristles against the light bulb that burned in the ceiling. 'Just unscrew the bulb and smash it and cut my wrists. That's what I ought to do. While you're still here. Somebody who cares about me a little bit.' "[11]

I was moved by Cullivan's character and this episode. Don Cullivan did care. He was concerned enough about Perry Smith and Perry's life with God to travel half the continent, spend needed money and use limited vacation time to help him.

The notion of care or concern, illustrated in a positive way by the incident with Don Cullivan, is also clarified when we look at a negative example such as the following which involves a young wife in her twenties:

Carolyn married at an early age and bore her husband several children. She grew restless, however, while her spouse was overseas on duty with the armed forces. She had occasional affairs with men about town, then finally took the children, left home and went to the West Coast. There she began to act very irresponsibly, living simultaneously in the same house with a number of men. She so neglected the care of her children that the civil authorities were forced to intervene and remove them from the house and from their mother. Legal interventions of this sort, as might be expected, come only when an extreme and intolerable situation exists. Later, before judge and husband, seeking to regain custody of the children despite the absence of any noticeable improvement in her conduct, Carolyn pleaded that she loved the children.

We would be quite ready to call her a liar.

Her lack of care and concern in such vital matters as food, clothing and protection signified that she in fact carried little true love in her heart for those children despite the vocal protestations.

The presence of care can signify real love; its absence is a sure sign that the love is false and insincere.

Openness

A second element common to all types of love is what we might best term *openness*. An open person responds to the needs of others. This responsiveness may be directed most obviously to a man's physical needs—to the poor person who seeks food or clothing, to the accident victim who requires immediate attention and assistance, to the blind man who struggles to cross the street. We can, of course, shut our hearts to these patent cases asking our open love. But it takes effort. It is a pretty cold, hardened human who can turn from such severe distress and go about his business. A responsive, open adult, however, becomes aware in addition of the deeper, less obvious needs of his fellow-man—those inner feelings which can bring more intense pain or joy to an individual than even the curse of a cancerous growth or the blessing of a large inheritance.

Openness means just that, being open to other people. Not closing our hearts to them, or to their lives. The closed person is all wrapped up in his own little world. He couldn't care less about the other fellow. Open love, like all self-giving love, demands some effort. A steel vice of self-centeredness constantly rings our hearts. It takes a day-after-day struggle to break out of its grasp. The battle to do so is a fluctuating one. One morning we rise and for some reason seem open, concerned, conscious of others and responsive to their needs and feelings. The next day a heavy cloud descends and suddenly there is only one world, mine, and only one set of significant problems, mine. It is an ongoing labor to love others openly.

For a half-dozen years I cared on a monthly basis for the religious needs of a little old lady confined to home and bed by age and illness. Marvin, her husband, displayed marvelous patience and concern during all those difficult years. It was necessary for him to feed and bathe her, to move his invalid wife whenever the bed required changing, to do all the cooking and cleaning. Sickness came eventually to Marvin also. The doctor ordered him to a local hospital for a hernia operation and his wife to a nursing home for special care during his recovery. She declined rapidly through these weeks and I was summoned one day to the old, large, converted mansion to administer the sacrament of the Anointing of the Sick. After I had completed my task and was leaving the convalescent home, a taxi pulled up and Marvin stepped out. I spoke to him about his wife's condition. He expressed regret that his weakened condition made it impossible to lift and thus to care for her adequately at home. Tears began to mount within him and I stretched my arm to his shoulder and tried to show some understanding by saying, "You miss her, don't you?"

Marvin never completed high school and spent his entire life on a farm. But lack of education in no way meant lack of affection for his dying wife. Tears streamed now and he sighed, "I miss her terrible."

Marvin is downcast, sad. His wife is about to die. That means separation, grief, loneliness. Any person who knows Marvin and loves him cannot remain closed and cold, unresponsive to his disconsolate state. The loving person must be open to this distraught man, doing his best to show that he understands, he feels with him, he shares his pain and trouble. This is openness.

Respect

A third element common to all forms of love is *respect*. Fromm explains its meaning: "Respect is not fear and awe; it denotes . . . the ability to see a person as he is, to be aware of his unique individuality. Respect means the concern that the other person should grow and unfold as he is. Respect, thus, implies the absence of exploitation. I want the loved person to grow and unfold for his own sake, and in his own ways, and not for the purpose of serving me. If I love the other person, I feel one with him or her, but with him *as he is*, not as I need him to be as an object for my use."[12]

The application of this notion of respect and love to the boy-girl courting relationship needs to be explored. Here again we pick up Noah Gordon's *The Rabbi*.

As a young man, Michael Kind spent the summer immediately after high school graduation on Cape Cod at the Hotel Sands near Falmouth, Massachusetts. It was there that he experienced his first deep emotional involvement with a woman. Ellen Trowbridge was the girl's name and she, like Michael, was working for the summer at the resort hotel and would enter college, Radcliffe, in the fall. Michael, Columbia bound, approvingly observed the waitress with "a good strong body that moved under her uniform when she walked, and thick yellow hair worn in a coil that made her look as though her picture belonged in an ad for Swedish beer." He finally found out her name by swallowing his pride and asking a fellow worker, Al Jenkins. He gave Michael little encouragement. "She's not your lollipop, Sonny boy," Jenkins said. "She's a frigid Radcliffe bitch who's strictly no-score. Ask the man who knows."

But Mike Kind was not exactly a hardened veteran at the game of chasing and conquering innocent young women. As a matter of fact, he had not even come close to scoring victory number one. Ellen attracted him. He pursued the matter and a wonderfully warm and intoxicating relationship eventually began to bloom. Early one morning, alone, on the beach, he began to do some things with her that he had never done before with any other girl. She cared for Michael but hesitated, even balked at his advances.

"Don't beg me," she said.

He grew angry. "What do you think I'm made of?" he said. "If you *really* loved me—"

"Don't you dare put that kind of price on us."[13]

Did Michael Kind respect Ellen Trowbridge in this incident? Or was he merely using her to satisfy his previously unsatisfied sexual curiosity? When she stopped his ardent efforts to become even more intimate and pleaded with him not to push so fast, or so hard, or so far, did his frustrated anger and argument indicate a lack of respect? Was he failing to take Ellen as she was, ignoring her own feelings and principles, allowing his inflamed passion to push him to ride roughshod over a girl who was at least half unwilling? It would be difficult, if not impossible, to answer those questions. But the very asking of them points out something about respect and love in the complicated relationship between a man and a woman.

It would be interesting to analyze the reaction of today's women to the question-title of this book, "Don't you really love me?" Certainly many young women have heard this as the sophisticated line of a male companion seeking to get what can be gotten. They often recognize the insincerity of the words and the request and reject them, gently or harshly as circumstances dictate. But others have heard it, no doubt, from sincere but confused adolescents who may be mixing up their urgent wish to learn and experiment with honest, tender feelings for the girl. Still others may have heard it from a man with whom they share a relationship of deep love. Does the girl questioned feel that the male questioner in every instance fails to show respect for her? In the first case it would be safe and fairly easy to respond affirmatively. Yes, he has failed to treat her as a person; he is using her. In the second instance, it could be difficult for her to determine the presence or the absence of respect. And in the third example, the judgment would be even more difficult and painful for her to make.

This notion of respect we have been discussing naturally applies to much more than the dating predicaments. Personal maturity of feeling, judgment and action demands a deep sense of respect for all other persons. Many individuals are extremely unhappy in life simply because they do not take other people as they are. They keep insisting that the other person conform to what he should be or what they want him to be. But life is complex and people are weak and countless factors contribute to make us the kind of persons we are. Peace and happiness in interpersonal relationships normally come only when we accept people as they are with both faults and virtues, with both pleasing personality traits and grating personal idiosyncrasies. Certainly marital success depends to a great extent upon acceptance and adjustment. We accept our partner as he or she is and we consequently adjust to those displeasing but unchangeable characteristics in the other member of the union. This again is respect for the other person, a respect which points to the presence of love.

An unconscious but real lack of respect frequently crops up in contemporary American homes. The young man or woman who wishes to marry, to leave home for college, to seek employment and housing away from his parents sometimes encounters stiff resistance. Such negative parental reaction can both surprise and depress the young person affected. Many reasons, of course, may bring on this disapproval but, at times, the root cause may be a lack of respect for the young adult. In effect, the parents are continuing to treat their son or daughter as a child, forgetting the fact that he or she is now a near or an actual adult. Parents should, ideally, allow the child gradually to unfold and develop as a mature, independent person. But those who fail to understand this or who seem unable to break the emotional cord binding them to their offspring may react negatively at these major moves removing the children from their protection and care. They have forgotten or do not grasp a parent's true role. True, honest respect, i.e., acceptance of the child as a developing, independent adult, is not present in their relationship. I would hesitate to say that means a lack of love. Rather, it would seem to denote the presence of misguided love.

Understanding

The fourth and final element common to all types of love is *understanding*. I do not mean understanding in the sense of objective knowledge about the world. A man may be a walking computer, filled with facts and figures about everything and everybody, yet still lack understanding and, consequently, love.

The understanding man I envision possesses a different aptitude. His understanding is more akin to wisdom, but still distinct from it. The understanding man goes beneath the surface of another person. His knowledge does not stop at the immediate, visible action or mood of the person he loves. He penetrates behind the external facade and discovers the true meaning of a particular act or expression.

Erich Fromm, who calls this type of understanding "knowledge," describes it as "one which does not stay at the periphery, but penetrates to the core."[14] Examples should clarify what I mean.

More and more the mystery of a happy marriage seems to rest on easy and honest communication between husband and wife. The lack of free-flowing discussion between the man and the woman often produces tensions, misunderstandings and, obviously, unhappiness. John has suffered serious setbacks in his work at the office. He is anxious about his domestic financial affairs, and the failure in that day's business dealings adds to his worry. He returns home tired, nervous and troubled. His wife greets him with a standard, but interested, "How were things at the office today?" John, like many men, tends to hide his anxieties within and prefers to keep them to himself until he has either solved them or is ready to discuss them with another, particularly his wife. He gives a sort of noncommittal answer to the question. His wife by this time reads John's mood more clearly and continues the questioning, "Is something wrong?" The husband replies with a terse and defensive, "No."

Trouble between John and his wife is in the infant

stage at this point. John wants to keep this within and may begin to resent her persistent prying to discover the cause of his obvious worry. His wife, on the other hand, feels that in marriage they should be sharing all things, including each other's problems. She sincerely wishes to know and possibly to help or at least comfort him in his difficulty. His rejection of her efforts or, better, his concealment from her of a very real anxiety thus may lead to a different resentment on the wife's part. A rather severe battle may even start over the question. Open communication which quickly brings to the surface those things which bother a partner in marriage often nips a misunderstanding like this before it can fester into serious disagreement and conflict.

But this communication must be oiled by understanding. John, for example, needs to penetrate beneath the surface of his wife's obvious curiosity and her search for information. He should recognize the love, the concern, the desire to share which prompt her questions. At the same time, his wife needs to understand why John is hesitant. She must recognize that his hesitation to reveal problems or to share them with her in no way signifies a lessening of the love he bears for her. It is rather for him a natural personality trait quite likely intensified by an unconscious urge to conform to the "strong, silent masculine stereotype." That male mystique judges it a sign of weakness for a man to reveal inner feelings, especially worries and fears. Years of living together in love can develop a couple's deep understanding of each other. The husband in time may understand her wish to share his inner life and hence try to fight the tendency to hide in his heart those deep emotions. In a similar fashion, the wife may come to understand his reticence. Love then prompts her to wait, to be patient until her husband is ready and willing to talk and communicate.

We all would be much happier in our relationships with others if we deeply grasped this notion of understanding and put it into practice. How often a classmate comes to school, a woman to work, a friend to lunch and acts or speaks in such a way as to inflict deep pain. The immediate reaction on our part is to think, "What did I do?" We may slip into a slight depression worrying about what we said or did to cause this action on the other person's part. The fact of the matter is that we are usually entirely innocent. We are generally in no way to blame for his or her bad mood and hurtful activity. Something went wrong for him or her at home, at school, at work; his health is poor, he is concerned about his job, his children are in trouble. Whatever the root reason he simply is taking it out on us. A love which includes understanding wisely sees this. If we are perceptive, and love can and should make us so, we gently seek to discover why a friend, a loved one, an associate acts in this troublesome way. It is not always easy to determine the fundamental cause. But we can in most cases judge quite quickly if we are the problem. And normally we are not. Once having absolved ourselves, it is helpful but not vitally important that we locate the true irritant. What is essential for love and understanding is that we go beneath the surface, restrain a natural reaction to "hurt back" and patiently put up with the other person.

What makes the whole business of understanding sometimes so difficult is the complex nature of man. Fromm comments, "While life in its merely biological aspects is a miracle and a secret, man in his human aspects is an unfathomable secret to himself—and to his fellowman."[15] We never really understand our own actions, much less those of others. That is to say, we never totally understand our own motives and, again, much less those of others. But to recognize that the actions of others on the surface are frequently deceptive, that deeper reasons lie behind the external word or deed, is the first and most significant step toward understanding. If we have that much understanding, we at least begin to grasp the complexity of human life and come to know a bit better and closer the "other fellow." And with this understanding which produces knowledge, we are in a position to love him.

St. Paul

I have maintained that the man who loves, gives; has concern for the person he loves; is open to his various needs; respects the person loved as he is, not as he should be or he wants him to be or he needs him to be; understands his words and actions. This consideration of love is, of course, general and basic. St. Paul, in his classical description of love from I Corinthians 13 expands somewhat that fundamental concept and sketches the ideal.

"Love is always patient and kind; it is never jealous; love is never boastful or conceited; it is never rude or selfish; it does not take offense, and is not resentful. Love takes no pleasure in other people's sins but delights in the truth; it is always ready to excuse, to trust, to hope, and to endure whatever comes.

"Love does not come to an end . . .

"In short, there are three things that last: faith, hope and love; and the greatest of these is love."[16]

Love is indeed a many-splendored thing. The aspects I have described in this chapter can apply to love between parent and child, husband and wife, friend and friend, priest and his people, employer and employee, even man and his God. The romantic relationship between a man and a woman, which we most commonly call love, must include all the elements mentioned above. But such romantic love goes beyond them. It becomes more specific. It adds a relationship between the opposite sexes. To appreciate this kind of sexual love we must first try to grow in our understanding of a man and a woman.

2. Men and Women Are

A n author grows and learns as he writes a book. I found this to be particularly true as I completed research for the present chapter.

Several years ago it was easy for me to be quite definite in my presentation of the differences between men and women: Men feel and react in this way, women in that. Then I began to read . . . and to lose some of my complacency. The subject is not all that simple.

While I have done considerable research, my observations here do not pretend to be exhaustive or scholarly. I hope they do show the complexity of the subject, as well as enable a young person to understand better his own sexuality and that of the opposite sex.

Such understanding and acceptance of sexuality demands that we avoid a false, stereotype "feminine mystique" and an equally dangerous but less publicized "male mystique." The following principles could, I think, aid in this.

1. *Treat each individual as a unique person.* Ignace Lepp succinctly states what has happened during the recent sexual or, better, the feminine revolution:

> "Not long ago women were very proud of their mission to be the servants of the species. Today they are conscious of themselves as *persons,* and desire for themselves all that goes along with being a person, namely, independence, freedom, the right to happiness and the right to individual development. Men have been animated for a long time by the same desires, but from now on they will not be able to satisfy these desires except in relation to those of their feminine companions."[1]

Earlier in his book, *The Psychology of Loving,* he brings out the mutual dependence of men and women:

> "Man and woman are indispensable to each other. They need each other and complete each other as two halves of one whole. This is evident

on the biological level. The propagation of the species requires the intimate cooperation of both sexes. . . . But the complementary nature of man and woman is equally unquestionable on the psychological plane as well. It seems to become more accentuated the more the human psyche evolves and becomes ever more complex and differentiated."[2]

Men and women, then, are persons, and complementary ones at that. In a way we are saying that men and women are equal but different. They help fulfill each other. Later on in this and in the next chapter I will discuss more in detail some examples of this mutual dependence operating in courtship and in the eventual selection of a marriage partner. But despite this mutual dependence, each man or woman remains a unique individual. As Demal notes, "It is of importance for the understanding of human souls to realize that each soul is unique and particular. No two souls of all the millions who have been created by God are exactly alike."[3] Myron Brenton makes a similar comment and links it with these false male and female stereotypes which need to be destroyed:

"The most important consideration is not whether most men are and do one thing and most women are and do another thing, but whether each person of either sex is recognized to be— and encouraged to be—unique unto himself. Society sets up its rules for what constitutes masculinity and femininity, but masculinity and femininity are after all just words, whereas human beings are not. Too, human beings have an enormous range of possibilities in terms of traits and in the ability to play roles of all kinds. These possibilities are severely foreshortened by the process of sex differentiation too rigidly applied and by masculinity and femininity too narrowly defined."[4]

To say men act and feel only in this way and that women act and feel only in that way sets up artificial compartments. It ignores the uniqueness of each person. It neglects the fact that there is an infinite variety of characteristics in human beings. Some men are very sensitive and open in their expressions of feelings even though perhaps most are not. Some women are unsatisfied in an exclusive role as housekeeper and childrearer even though many or most may find fulfillment in these tasks. But to say you are less a man because you are sensitive or less a woman because you want a career is just not true. Brenton describes how cruel and unfortunate such rigid categorizing can be:

"It's one thing to state that every person contains both masculine and feminine components. This is just a different way of asserting that every person has the potential to express all the traits we now ascribe separately to each sex, with society stressing some characteristics at the expense of others. It's quite another thing to say in effect, 'You're a sensitive intuitive man? Brother, there must be a lot of woman in you. You're an artist? A writer? A minister? A psychologist? Brother, the female is showing!'

"To label as feminine traits like sensitivity, intuition, and the capacity to understand people is to fit the male into a masculine straitjacket."[5]

The author is talking about the American male and the false stereotypes which we establish for him. There are equally cruel and injurious stereotypes for the American female. Betty Friedan examines them in her book, *The Feminine Mystique*.

The solution, in my opinion, is to treat each person as a unique individual. But this demands an openness to people as persons, an awareness of some false notions we entertain about the way men and women supposedly should act, and courage and initiative to be ourselves and treat others as they really are.

Let me illustrate what this theoretical discussion can mean in a practical way. John Wayne is not the only model for men—tough, aggressive, strong, silent, leave-it-all-down-in-the-guts type. There are men, many of them, like him. But there are other men who are more gentle, who are sensitive to others, who easily express their feelings. One type is not more a man than the other. They are both men, but differ from each other. So too the busy-around-the-house-surrounded-by-my-children type is not the only model for women. Again, many if not most women are content with this role. But others want careers, dare to practice medicine and even to study physics. The one who opts in this way is not less a woman. These are two more obvious instances of false masculine and feminine straitjackets. There are others.

2. *Be your natural self.* This flows very logically from the lengthy preceding material. If we are unique individuals with particular talents, training and traits, then we should establish our own personal identity and live according to it. The discovery of our own identity, however, is an arduous and not always successful task. It is also a constant and ever-changing one. It takes a long time for a man to really know himself, to know the kind of person he is. And then he is not sure he has discovered the real self. But as time moves on and we grow, learn and mature, some of our more obvious characteristics become clear. We then need to accept them and adjust to people and society as is necessary.

This is a certain type of role playing. We need to find out what is our honest, true role in life based on the characteristics we have inherited, our training in life and the evironment in which we live. Then we try to live according to that role. What is not natural and true to the real self is a conformity to certain unduly tight rules and attitudes that society says we should follow. This is false role playing.

The husband who conceals his inner anxieties from his wife simply because the role of the male in marriage is to be strong and silent is following a false role and not the one his true self wishes to follow. The woman college graduate who avoids adult education courses and outside activities merely because the female's role is supposedly in the home is not in harmony with her true self, but merely conforming to an artificial role.

3. *Do not exaggerate the woman's role as child-*

bearer and housekeeper. This is not to deny the dignity of a woman as wife and mother. Nor is it to ignore the fact that many women do find satisfaction and fulfillment in raising a family and keeping a home. Feminists like Betty Friedan, I think, must be careful lest in their protest against stringent female stereotypes they go to the opposite extreme and cast aspersion on the wife and mother who is honestly and sincerely very happy with her position.

Still, times have changed. Women live longer. Menopause in past cultures was no serious problem. Not many women ever reached that age. Today the childbearing and -rearing years of a woman consume only a portion of her life. Will she be satisfied with only a mother's role? What about those years in later life? What is her function, her value, her identity then?

Times have changed, too, in housekeeping. The mechanical age has made it possible to clean the house and cook the meals in much less time. Every hour of the day in former years was needed in order to eke out an existence. But this is not always true in modern society. The woman who is finished in a few moments may wonder what need she fulfills in life. Is there something more to life and her life than housekeeping?

Times have changed intellectually or, to be more accurate, educationally. More and more women hold college degrees and have been exposed to the intellectual life. They enjoy motherhood. They find certain satisfaction in maintaining a warm, clean, pleasant home. But they still experience the call of the spirit, a need to continue reading, studying, learning. I recently visited with a married woman, mother of three, wife of a civil engineer. A college graduate, she is presently working on a master's degree in library science. However, she attends class only once or twice a week. The deep reason for this continued education is not the degree nor a desire to work and supplement the family income nor a wish to develop her ability to support the children independently in case of a future emergency. The real reason is her need to read, study and learn.

Unfortunately, the picture of today's woman has not

kept up with the changing times. Betty Friedan describes the image:

> "The image of woman that emerges from this big, pretty magazine is young and frivolous, almost childlike; fluffy and feminine; passive; gaily content in a world of bedroom and kitchen, sex, babies, and home. The magazine surely does not leave out sex; the only passion, the only pursuit, the only goal a woman is permitted is the pursuit of a man. It is crammed full of food, clothing, cosmetics, furniture, and the physical bodies of young women, but where is the world of thought and ideas, the life of the mind and the spirit? In the magazine image, women do not work except housework and work to keep their bodies beautiful and to get and keep a man."[6]

She does not like this image. Her book was written to show that there is great restlessness in the hearts of American women, that the mother and housekeeper role seems no longer adequate for today's female. She states her case in this paragraph:

> "It is my thesis that the core of the problem for women today is not sexual but a problem of identity—a stunting or evasion of growth that is perpetuated by the feminine mystique. It is my thesis that as the Victorian culture did not permit women to accept or gratify their basic sexual needs, our culture does not permit women to accept or gratify their basic need to grow and fulfill their potentialities as human beings, a need which is not solely defined by their sexual role."[7]

As I understand this contention, we can no longer limit the model woman to a role as wife and mother and housekeeper. This is part of a woman's role, a fine, beautiful, important part. One woman will find this alone sufficient for personal fulfillment. But another will not be so content and will feel the need to go beyond husband, home and children. This does not mean she ignores or neglects him or them. It means, rather, she develops a supplement to the wife-mother role.

For the single girl this new understanding of women offers some hope of satisfaction and identity instead of relegation to the customarily forlorn lot of spinster, old maid, "poor girl who never got married." Because times have changed and our attitudes are in the process of being altered, it seems to me an important principle that we not overstress the so-called traditional woman's "role" and thus restrict any woman to the position of wife, mother and housekeeper.

Differences

This stress on the uniqueness of the individual personality, the equality between sexes, the need for naturalness and honesty with oneself, the avoidance of false male and female stereotypes—all these emphases may seem to deny existing differences between sexes. This is not my purpose at all. Men and women are different. But it would seem we have gone slightly astray in determining why and how they differ. Priest and psychiatrist Ignace Lepp comments, "Remaining strictly on the level of psychological observation, we can state that in practice the majority of women are 'feminine' and the majority of men 'masculine.' The line of demarcation, however, is really less rigid than it is customarily conceived to be."[8]

Just how much the differences are biological and stem from purely physical, inherited factors and how much they are cultural and stem from the environment and society in which we live is not easy to ascertain. Myron Brenton summarizes well what I am trying to say:

"This is not to suggest that no differences between men and women exist other than those culturally determined. The physical differences are gloriously and unchangingly apparent. The differences in biological functioning are not to be denied. To say that biological differences create no psychological differences would be absurd; every woman knows how different she feels at various stages in her life—during pregnancy, for instance, or after her baby has been born. She's acutely aware, before she becomes a mother, of the potentialities for creation of human life inside her body. She knows the changes in mood and feeling that she goes through before and during menstruation (although some women claim to go through none at all). But how much of this is innate and how much is result of cultural conditioning remain questions. . . . No one can say precisely where biology leaves off and culture begins."[9]

Having placed all this in proper perspective, we can now move on and investigate just what are these specific biological and psychological differences. I presume that my reader by this time has read, heard or seen an explanation of the fundamental biological "facts of life." The presumption may be erroneous in some instances, but I would like to think that all or the vast majority have received at least that much instruction in sex.

Biological Differences

It is common to separate these biological differences into several categories. The *primary* sexual characteristics deal with the very organs of reproduction. For the man these are the testicles, the two organs which produce the semen or sperm. For the woman these are the ovaries, the two organs which produce the ova or eggs. The *secondary* sexual characteristics deal with the organs directly concerned with copulation, gestation and nutrition. The latter two activities are exclusively feminine. For copulation, the organs are the vulva and the vagina for the woman and the penis for the man. For gestation the proper organ is the uterus or womb and for nutrition the specific organs are the breasts. It is significant to note here that in the male the breasts are atrophic because they have no function and in the female they are larger because they are functional.

All other differentiating characteristics are grouped under *tertiary* sexual characteristics. Here the nice, neat differences begin to vanish. We enter into the complex world in which there is a crossing, a blending of male and female traits. It is not easy or possible, in some instances, to determine what is strictly physical, biological and what is cultural. Thus we encounter microscopic chromosomes. We face the question of male hormones (androgens) and female hormones (estrogens). A preponderance of one over the other causes a man to have male characteristics and a woman, female traits. There is, therefore, something of the man in each woman and something of the woman in each man.

We face the facts that men are physically stronger, more heavily built, more muscular, have more heavily built skeletons, are taller, possess a pelvis which is heavier, higher, more funnel-shaped, more heavily muscled with a pubic arch or angle whose aperture varies from 70-75 degrees. Women, in contrast, are physically weaker, less heavily built, have lighter skeletal structures, are smaller, possess a pelvis designed to facilitate the passage of the baby through the birth canal and which is, therefore, lighter, lower, more graceful, less conical, less heavily muscled with a pubic arch which varies from 90 to 100 degrees—a broader pelvis, therefore, which shows itself in her more rounded hips.

These differences in cellular structure, hormone content and anatomical composition seem to exercise an influence on the behavior of men and women. At least there is evidence of this from the investigation of little children, presumably before cultural pressures might sway them into distinct patterns. Howard J. Osofsky, M.D., associate professor in the Department of Obstetrics and Gynecology at the Upstate Medical Center in Syracuse, listed some interesting facts in his talk on "Femaleness—A Genetic or Environmental Determination?" at a symposium I recently attended. Studies indicate that male children differ from female children in behavior also. Thus the small boy appears more active, restless, aggressive. He manifests inward tension by bed-wetting and tics. The young girl, on the other hand, shows earlier muscular coordination, more deft hand movements, a greater interest in clothes, a swifter ability to dress herself. She tends to manifest her inward tension by nail biting and thumb sucking. She at this early age appears more shy than her male counterpart and, outwardly, seems to be more the quiet, well-behaved child.

Yet even here one can question the validity of these investigations on several premises. To reiterate what Brenton says, "No one can say precisely where biology leaves off and culture begins." But, in practice, I am not sure it is all that important for the young man or woman for whom I am writing this book.

Psychological Differences

It seems to me relatively unimportant to determine why we feel, think, act differently as men or women. Why? Because the American man I meet in the street is a product of his age and culture. He was born a man with distinguishing primary and secondary and some tertiary characteristics. He has received a particular training from parents, school, community. He has felt and continues to feel the vast cultural pressures of his time, some obvious, others more subtle. He stands before me now. I must deal with him as an individual. There has never been another man exactly like him, nor is there anyone like him now, nor will there ever be another man like him in the future. To sift and sort why he is like he is does not seem so consequential; to accept him and love him as he is does seem important.

It can be helpful, however, for young people to be aware of the more evident psychological traits in the contemporary male and female. The following sketches are to be interpreted strictly in terms of the limitations we talked about: there is no concrete, "average" man (or woman).

The American Man

1. *Is aggressive and competitive.* In our culture the young male learns from early childhood that he lives in a rough, tough world. He quickly must face the fact that life is competitive. Get the job done, be aggressive, search and kill, produce or else, win, BEAT 'EM, the crowd shouts, be first, never rest with second place—he hears phrases like these over and over again. This

begins in the games preschoolers play, continues with Little League, grows more intense during the teen-age years and remains steady, persistent although more refined in adulthood.

The young American man realizes that he must produce or someone else will take his place on the team, in school, in society, at work. He visualizes and is given his future role as protector and provider. That means working and earning and also doing a bit better than the other fellow. It means being a doer more than a thinker.

The world around him is seen as something to be studied and conquered for his use and for the benefit of those who depend upon him. In this sense the man sees himself as creative in subduing the earth. Demal concludes from all this that man is more creative than woman and cites as proof the fact that nearly all inventions and discoveries as well as the major works of art are the product of a man's genius, not a woman's. Contemporary feminists question this assertion and ask if such data does not instead reflect and result from the repression of women in past history. Given an equal opportunity, perhaps women would have presented the world with equivalent advances in science, technology and the fine arts.

The male role to protect wife, to provide for her and the children she bears him is still very much in evidence among American men. One young man talked to me recently about his own feelings in church on the day of his wedding. He admits he is not an overly religious person and does not hesitate to acknowledge he "had been around" in his early youth. This man felt as he walked down the aisle that he was "simply going with the girl." When he walked out of the church following the nuptial vows, he told me he felt completely different. Now he sensed that this girl was his wife and his responsibility. Now he had the obligation of caring for her and providing for her needs. Such a role and image tends to make the male more aggressive since he must earn in a fiercely competitive world the money which feeds the children, houses the family, clothes the youngsters, supplies their education, and pays the premiums on expensive insurance policies which will protect them should he, their provider and protector, suddenly be removed from the home.

Dr. Cavanaugh makes this male role as father of the house and head of the family a natural position for the man:

"Nature confirms this designation of the husband as the leader in the home by giving him greater strength, a natural ability in leadership and government, and in the fact that his fatherhood does not interfere with his duties in support of the family. The mother, on the other hand, is more frail, has a natural tendency to be dependent and is necessarily so at times because of motherhood. The husband is recognized by the wife as the natural leader because no woman would want to be married to a man she could not admire, upon whom she could not depend, and whom she would not desire to be the father of her children. These statements should not be interpreted to indicate 'female inferiority.' Men and women are different, not unequal. Each sex has been assigned by nature to perform a specialized role."[10]

I think Betty Friedan, Sidney Callahan and Myron Brenton might object in some degree to these remarks by Dr. Cavanaugh.

Contemporary society still sees man as aggressive in the sexual realm, that is, in the dating and courtship area. The image of the male on the make trying to seduce some innocent young virgin is common enough. So, too, is the picture of the man on the prowl seeking to devour some willing and probably not-so-innocent female. The very title of this book, "Don't You Really Love Me?" projects that notion. It is the boy who generally asks the question. He is the one who is seeking to go further. The girl normally is the one who must respond. She is judged to be the one who keeps matters under control, who fights off her insistent companion.

I could go on at some length exploring this point. For example, one wonders if, at times, the girl is not the subtle aggressor, playing a game, leading her male companion on so he asks this question. Or one conjectures if she actually wants him to ask the question, even though she very likely will respond, "Yes, but," and answer "No" to his urgent pleas. The frequently drawn picture of the man as the big, bad, dirty fellow who is interested only in physical sex and in using any and every girl (the Alfie image) surely can be overdrawn. At the same time, it is the boy who usually asks the girl for a date and who proposes marriage. And it is the young man who kisses his girl and the young woman who "lets her boyfriend kiss her." Only later, normally, will she "kiss him back."

2. *Needs to feel superior.* Leo Durocher's famous managerial comment on baseball ("Nice guys always finish last.") says something about the success mania which prevails in modern America. Everyone loves a winner; few follow the loser. The top team takes the trophies; the "also-rans" are soon forgotten. This holds true not only for competitive sports but also for nearly every facet of contemporary life. The American male breathes in such an atmosphere and it helps create within him a need to feel superior, if not in all ways, at least in some.

The anxiety to feel superior manifests itself early enough in the young boy's language and conversation. He swears a lot, brags, acts terribly conceited. Later he may display this need when he eats and drinks in great, sometimes excessive, quantities. He may even seek to dominate and conquer a young woman in an aggressive, sexual manner. In all of these situations, the man may be trying, although usually quite unconscious of what he is doing and why, to prove that he is superior, the king, the conqueror.

No doubt this need, coupled with physical strength and competitive spirit, explains the great interest many young men have in athletics. For them it is not always simply a matter of fun, a leisure-time activity. It may be a test of their superiority. Joan Salvato, the champion lady fly caster of the world, commented on this attitude in an interview quoted in Brenton's book:

"When a man sets about learning a new

sport, he feels he has to prove himself. He feels he has to be, if not the greatest, at least very good. If he doesn't pick it up right away, he's impatient and insecure. When a woman takes up a sport, she doesn't have to prove herself. She's proved herself with children and a house—or, if not married, by just being a woman who isn't expected to be a great sportsman."[11]

Is this why a young woman might notice her boy-friend's depressed, almost irked feelings after she defeated him on the bowling lanes? Or, more subtly, is this why a girlfriend might deliberately allow her partner to win in miniature golf or cards or in some other game?

The need for a feeling of superiority also may explain men's intense interest as spectators in sports. A man may become elated at his team or his favorite player's success and grow sullen at his team or player's failure. There is a vicarious conquest or defeat here for the male spectator. He identifies with the team or the player. When they win, he wins; when they lose, he loses. I must confess that I never personally understood why I felt sad when my favorite baseball team (the Phillies) lost until I began to study this aspect of psychology.

This particular attitude may also explain why some men feel that their future wives should not be as well educated, as intelligent, as cultured, as wealthy as they are. It also explains why many husbands keep important decision-making matters, especially financial ones, to themselves. It also helps to unravel the frequently observed phenomenon that some, if not most, men tend to keep their feelings hidden. I will discuss this particular attitude in a moment.

I am not, of course, insisting that the need to feel superior is a particularly virtuous and praiseworthy attribute. I am simply, if you recall my earlier principles, remarking that the American man generally tends to possess this characteristic.

3. *Grows discouraged more easily.* Some writers see this trait as a man's most serious psychological weakness. Statistics indicate, apparently, that three

out of four suicides are men, that nine out of 10 alcoholics are men, that the majority of school dropouts, prescinding from pregnancies, are men. A man generally grows discouraged unless he is making progress, meeting with success, receiving recognition. I feel myself that every individual needs constant encouragement, especially in our depersonalized contemporary culture. But it seems that men particularly do demand it.

This fact has obvious practical significance for the girlfriend, fiancée and wife. Her role frequently may be one of inspiration and restoration — making her husband or lover sense that he is important, valuable, a success at least in his position at home or with her. Later on in this book I will cite an example from a modern novel in which a wife, through sensitive concern and lovemaking, is able to relieve her husband's anxiety and depression over a business clash and to restore his sense of importance as an individual.

4. *Deals with generalities, tends to ignore details.* In the customary role as provider and protector, the American male necessarily sees himself struggling with huge and vital concerns. Concerned as a lawyer with a $40,000 paternity suit or as an engineer with a construction estimate running into the millions, he may judge as insignificant or needless his wife's anxiety about penny savings at the supermarket or her worry over the youngest son's slight misconduct in school. He fights and works and schemes to provide his wife and family with food and security and a good home and the opportunity for a college education. Since he does this well and conscientiously, the man may feel his task is finished. The emotional needs of the family, he thinks, are not his province nor his responsibility.

Little things can mean much to the wife—the anniversary dinner, the birthday present, the Valentine card, the morning kiss good-bye. The modern man may overlook those things, forget them and thus precipitate a major crisis in family relations. It is not really lack of care that brings this neglect for such details, but more a preoccupation with what he terms the overall picture, the really big problems and challenges he daily faces. The wife, on the other hand, may interpret his forgetfulness as a sign that their mutual love is on the wane and she may grow discouraged, depressed, tearful or angry.

5. *Reasons logically and objectively.* Facing the hard-nosed "world" outside the home, the man's mind seeks the truth, deals with reality, wants logical answers and reasoned conclusions. The American male can grow irked when his female partner simply and suddenly sweeps all arguments aside and decides for some inexplicable, intuitive reason that this is the right thing. "Why?" the man asks. "I don't know why. I just know." Ashley Montagu, in his dashing, inimitable way, asserts that this merely proves the woman's intelligence is superior to the man's. A man, he says, laboriously reasons to a conclusion; a woman quickly arrives at the point through intuition.

6. *Keeps feelings inside.* Myron Brenton explains well this particular male characteristic, its origin, and its effect upon the man and his female associates, especially his wife.

"To be sure, men are much less stoic than they ever were in the past. There has been a considerable loosening up. The American male is much more able today to talk about his insecurities than he was before. But to acknowledge this is not to contradict the fact that the image of the strong silent male even now has a great deal of relevance among all classes and all age groups of American men. When Dr. Mirra Kimarovsky asked the husbands in her blue-collar study what subjects they would be reluctant to discuss with their wives, their answers include the following: anything having to do with the job; financial worries; hurt feelings and aggravations having to do with friends and relatives; hopes, dreams, and dissatisfactions (anything having to do with man's inner core); any gripes the men had about their wives; and things they were told confidentially.

"A pretty good case could be made for encouraging men to unburden themselves at times —both from the standpoint of the deepening communication that would result between themselves and their spouses and from the standpoint of mental health, for what he holds back may eventually erupt in the form of psychosomatic and other disorders. But that isn't the purpose here. The purpose is simply to suggest that the masculinity trap is a needless constriction, that a male is neither a superior man for always keeping silent about troubles nor an inferior man for candidly discussing them with his wife. The 'strong silent' stereotype has as its source not an impulse to protect women but male vanity—vanity that says, 'You can't see me hurt or distraught, for that would destroy the image of my invincible self, which I must always present to you'; vanity that says, in the pathetically honest (and wistful) words of a Harvard student quoted in *Sex and the College Girl,* 'Women tell men how women feel. It just pours out. But men have to go out and get drunk before they open up. Otherwise, it isn't manly.' Nor can the manly American male ever find release in tears, though men in many other nations are not so constrained."[12]

The modern American girl, it seems to me, can use Brenton's observations as an aid in determining how well her friendship and love-relationship with an individual man is progressing. Since many men do tend to conceal their feelings, the boy or man who gradually begins to open up and reveal his inner hopes and anxieties, his aspirations and fears must have confidence in the woman to whom he bares his heart. He trusts her and is beginning to have some special feeling for her. Their future together has some possibilities.

7. *The man is more quickly aroused physically and sexually.* There can be sexual arousal (especially in a woman) without a concomitant genital excitation. However, we mean here a strictly genital arousal. It seems generally verified that men are more swiftly aroused and more quickly satisfied. Women as a rule are excited more slowly and their excitation is slower to subside and extends over a longer period. In addition,

as a substantiation of this characteristic, statistics will appear later on in another context indicating a higher incidence of masturbation in men than in women.

Hettlinger summarizes some pertinent findings by Kinsey:

> "Women are far less aroused by psychological stimuli to sexual excitement than men are. The average male is readily excited by the thought of coitus; and as soon as a relationship becomes at all intimate, he tends to think in these terms, thus compounding the pressure toward sexual fulfillment. But the average girl, certainly if she is sexually inexperienced, is likely neither to engage in fantasies of coitus nor to be stimulated erotically by such thoughts. Kinsey made a careful and interesting study of thirty-three kinds of erotic psychological stimulation by which the majority of men are affected. These included nude pictures, the genitalia of the other sex, burlesque and floor shows, animals and humans in coitus, erotic stories, lavatory drawings, and discussions about sex. He discovered that the majority of women were largely uninterested in and unaroused by such things. The only two items that produced comparable interest among women were motion pictures (not specifically pornographic) and 'literary materials' (i.e., novels, essays, and poetry). And in both these instances, as Kinsey noted, it may well be the romantic element rather than the explicitly sexual content, which appeals to the woman. But in any case it is obvious that factors leading to intense sexual stimulation in the man may leave his partner cold."[13]

This list of traits commonly found in American men is not an exhaustive grouping. It includes merely the more apparent ones and those which exercise a frequent and significant influence upon the relationship between men and women. As I now sketch a few major characteristics of American women, it should be obvious that the comments will need to be related to the foregoing and sometimes overlapping material.

The American Woman

1. *Manifests capacity for endurance.* To say that a man is stronger than a woman restricts the meaning of strength to brute power. For a woman, generally speaking, displays strength in another fashion—an ability to endure pain and suffering for extended periods of time. Ashley Montagu would claim this proves the naturally superior strength of women and cites in support two interesting facts. Women tend to live longer than men. For example, it is a safe bet, Montagu maintains, to wager that in quintuplets the female infants will survive longer than the male babies. An even more fascinating illustration touches the World War II air raids in London. A postwar study of psychiatric problems resulting from these intense bombings shows that for every one woman who suffered a mental breakdown there were 70 similar collapses on the part of men.

It is sometimes stated that a man can endure extremely intense pain, although only for a short interval. A woman will faint or grow hysterical in the face of such a severe blow. On the other hand, a man, confronted with a long siege of suffering, will find it most difficult to resign himself to this fate. A woman, meeting a similar kind of difficulty, seems to bear and accept the burden more easily. One could see this as a preparation by nature for the extended hardships a woman faces in pregnancy. She can endure these with relative placidity; a man probably would bear them less graciously.

My pastoral experience as a priest sees this woman's trait manifested on occasion in the instance of a wife's dogged loyalty to an unfaithful husband or to a disappointing child. She seems to have a capacity to wait, to understand, to bear with it all—always hoping the husband will reform and return to his home and her heart, always believing the prodigal son or daughter will eventually regain balance and come to his or her senses. How much this is a social phenomenon, merely a resignation to situations beyond her control and a sort of saving face with her associates, remains a good question.

2. *More disposed to love.* The American woman

seems to bear within her a strong desire to give, to yield totally to some person or some cause, to surrender herself unconditionally to someone or something. As proof of that greater urge to love, one author notes that religious nuns and sisters outnumber priests in the United States by a two-to-one margin. Often for the woman love is everything. The comment is frequently made, rightly or wrongly, that the man wants sex, the woman seeks love. I have experienced in counseling young adults the occasional readiness of a woman, once assured of a boyfriend's or fiancé's love, to cast aside suddenly all previous sexual standards, codes, moral rules and to give herself in a total physical way. Later, she may wonder at the overwhelming power love had at that time in altering her previous attitudes.

Certainly the period of conception, pregnancy and birth demands an unusual amount of love. The infant within the mother's womb is dependent upon her self-giving for life and growth. The same can be said for the child in early years—it looks to the mother for food, protection, security, warmth and love. The mother is called upon by her very role to give totally of herself. Our society expects that of a mother and we shudder at extreme examples of neglect, coldness and lack of love.

Needless to say, love in itself is a highly desirable trait. Whether a woman is more disposed to love than a man, as described here, is highly controversial. If it is true, then it simply means the man needs to envy his female companion and should strive to imitate this particularly good characteristic of the woman.

3. *Can hate more easily.* If a woman's strength is to love, then it can equally be asserted that her weakness is a propensity to hate. Men grow angry, fight, and forget. Women become irked, conceal their resentment under a facade of graciousness, carry a grudge and nurse a hatred. I have watched my young male basketball players exchange angry words, punches and threats of various sorts during the heat of battle. Later, after the game, the same warring athletes walk from the gymnasium the best of friends. At the same time, a young woman may silently smolder for weeks and

months and finally erupt into some overtly hostile action toward a fellow female. The reason—her adversary had been friendly and flirtatious with a boyfriend.

4. *Tends to be religious*. The observation has been made that Italian churches are filled—but only with women. The man works; the woman worships. This does not seem to hold true in American Catholicism. At least there is a better ratio between men and women churchgoers. Still, something can be said to the effect that even the contemporary woman seems more religious than her male counterpart. Demal would see this as a natural consequence of the psychic disposition. The man finds it difficult, he maintains, to love with all his heart and to give himself without reserve. Since he cannot, in practice, abandon himself to God there is a certain soberness, an impersonal and abstract aspect in his relationship with God. Prayer is more for him a type of thinking rather than loving with a resultant weakness in commitment and in the ability to sacrifice.

Caffarel links this to woman's closeness with nature and the rhythm of life. He also sees man's aggressive, decision-making trait and his need to feel superior as impediments to deep religious habits. He argues that the woman is more naturally religious. The spontaneous impulse of her feminine personality enables her to love husband and God completely, with utter abandon. She can humble herself before God and submit to His will without great pain. But the man, in Caffarel's view, must do an about-face. To be submissive may strike him, particularly in the beginning, as contrary to his masculine role. His wife's habits and attitudes may lead him slowly to make the necessary adjustments and to develop some deep and steady religious habits.

I am not sure how I stand on this issue. I have known in a dozen years as a priest many devout men. But I have also known numerically more religious women. And throughout the course of assisting over 250 couples in their marriage preparations I have witnessed many instances of religious renewal in a man stemming largely from the woman's example and her faithful dedication to God and Church. How much is natural and how much is a matter of cultural factors remains, for me, a mystery.

5. *Concerned with details.* I have covered this trait earlier under a consideration of the man's tendency to ignore minute matters and to concentrate on the bigger issues. The role of the woman as mother demands love, as I mentioned, but it also requires attentiveness to small details—the baby's formula, the proper medicine, the correct sizes for clothes.

The concern some women show for small but meaningful gestures (cards, flowers, phone call) may be traced, one wife told me, to the female's need to feel appreciated. The wife who sobbingly calls the office and wonders if her husband still loves her because he neglected to kiss her good-bye in the morning very likely knows he does, but is hurt because his neglect of a detail makes her feel she is being taken for granted. At least she interprets his oversight in that way.

A young girl, it seems to me, enjoys the date who takes her to a hamburger stand on his Honda but who notices and appreciates her as a person in many small ways. She enjoys him, that is, more than the rich young man with the Thunderbird who takes her to dinner at a plush restaurant and a floor show at an exclusive night club but who never really notices her, never really appreciates how she looks, never comments on what she is wearing or what she is like as a person.

Is it true, as one writer suggested, that a husband fears most this one question when he arrives home from work: "Darling, do you notice anything new?"

6. *Thinks intuitively.* This relates to the earlier discussion of a man's tendency to reason, to arrive at conclusions after a laborious struggle. The woman seems to grasp the situation spontaneously. A vivid imagination can color her reasoning powers. The man deals with here-and-now facts that can be measured in terms of immediate results. The woman, on the other hand, goes beyond that. She treasures values that seem more "eternal" and less tangible—love, goodness, pity, protection, beauty. Because subjective and emotional

factors easily can sway her reason, it seems to a man that she is biased in certain decisions.

7. *Passive.* This corresponds in part to the aggressive characteristic of the male counterpart. Many girls and women seem to want to be led, to be subservient, to have the man and male lead, make the decisions, be the head of the house. This affects all aspects of those women's lives, including the physically sexual relationship between husband and wife, man and woman.

As I have discussed earlier, it seems, from a genital point of view, that the female does tend to be less easily excitable. Later on in another chapter, I will comment on how this can and sometimes does change as a love and dating relationship deepens and develops. It does appear, however, that the girl's main concern often is with romance, affection, caring, security, protection, and that she finds necking, petting, intercourse desirable only insofar as they bear some connection with these other values. Hettlinger notes: "For the man, advanced petting or intercourse is likely to be desirable, whether his feeling for the girl is deep or not. For her it is more likely to be unattractive or even repugnant if no romantic relationship exists. If she finds the man attractive and enjoys his company, the girl will accept further intimacies, not because she desires them but because he does and she wants to please him."[14]

A few paragraphs later the same author summarizes all this and remarks that in the present age, the average responsible girl regards sex without love and affection as a "bore and a waste."

8. *Possesses a readiness to express in feelings and experiences a greater fluctuation in her moods.* Myron Brenton, in a quotation appearing earlier in this chapter, commented on the changes in mood and feeling that a woman experiences during menstruation. In addition to this monthly variation in her emotional life, it seems that the cycle of elation and depression for a woman is more pronounced than that for a man. This kind of statement, of course, is difficult to confirm on any scientific basis but what does appear more certain on the surface is the greater ease with which women

express their feelings. They cry. Men, as I have noted, feel, at least some of them, that they must choke back their tears. Ashley Montagu sees this as a further substantiation of the woman's superiority. He contends that she uses her emotions in a natural way and that man artificially tries to suppress them.

It is also observed that women seem to sense quickly other people's moods and feelings. Men may ignore these, or better, not recognize such subtle and semi-hidden tensions and attitudes. This trait can cause pain in the woman but it also enables her to offer compassion and understanding and to show great sensitivity. Female sensitiveness came up for discussion one evening at a convent in a lengthy visit I had with several of the sisters. They felt that as women they sensed quickly the ups and downs of other sisters living a close community life in the same house. This enables them, they thought, to support one another in sorrows and to share effectively one another's joys.

Such intuitiveness on the emotional as well as the intellectual level may explain why so often men are confused or irked at the seemingly inexplicable behavior of women. It is because the man fails to realize adequately the woman's own feelings and her swift perception of the feelings of others. He thus cannot understand her consequent actions or her subsequent moods.

* * * *

This chapter should, I think, stimulate the reader, provoke some conversation between couples, and promote classroom discussion. The matter is controversial. And it does foster self-questioning. Am I like this? Does my boyfriend, my girlfriend, my wife, my husband react in this way? Am I being true to myself or am I only conforming to some false role? If it does impel the reader to think and to ask himself or herself some of these and other related questions, then it has achieved its purpose.

The richness of the individual personality and the marvelously fascinating blend of the male and female in persons living today means we will never arrive at definitive answers to these questions. But the very fact that we may now recognize the complexity of the male-female relationship means growth, maturation, understanding. Perhaps the best attitude to take is to evaluate traits apart from their maleness or femaleness and judge them to be desirable or undesirable, as the case may be. Thus to be sensitive, to love, to express feelings naturally, to be logical, to lead reason-directed lives, to be ambitious and aggressive in a nonexploitative way, to be religious — these strike me as highly beneficial qualities in every person. On the contrary, to hate, to be blinded by emotions, to show overconcern for minute details, to submit slavishly to another, to dominate those we meet, to need a false sense of superiority, to hide our emotions artificially, to be cold and insensitive to the total feelings of others — these appear to me as traits every individual should try to eliminate from his life. We complement one another as men and women. The task at hand may be to learn from one another, to imitate the good qualities of the other of whatever sex.

* * * *

Tony Wood thinks he is in love with a woman; Ann Phillips thinks she is in love with a man. But it isn't just *any* woman or *any* man. It is this particular woman and this particular man. To know that you truly love one person you must understand not only something about love in general, not only something about men and women and their similarities and differences, but you must also understand what can be special and singular about this individual man, this individual woman.

3. Picking Your Partner

In 1935, Carlo Levi, a doctor, painter, philosopher, and man of letters, was forced by the Fascists to live as a political prisoner in the barren province of Lucania, in southern Italy. He wrote a book, *Christ Stopped at Eboli,* describing his year in the midst of an impoverished people who lived in a desolate land surrounded by death. In the final chapter of the work, Levi illustrates the process of an "arranged marriage" so foreign to us in the United States, but not unheard of in other countries.

Giulia, a central figure in the book, had borne her first son 20 years earlier. The boy's father abandoned Giulia almost immediately and took the child with him to Argentina. Later, after growing up, the young man volunteered for service with the Italian army in Abyssinia. Giulia heard from the boy occasionally and one day a note of particular importance arrived.

The war, her son mentioned, would soon be over and he pleaded with his mother to find him a wife in Gagliano. He would be quite content with her selection of a future mate and would marry the girl she chose as soon as he came back to his home town. He had left the village at a very early age, far too young to remember anything about it, much less recall the girls who lived there. Thus he proposed to return to a place he had never seen, to marry a woman he had never known. His mother, accustomed to that sort of procedure, complied with the request, selected a bride for him, and the two, mother and future daughter-in-law, settled down for the boy's return and the wedding day.

We do things differently in America. We pick our own partners. And love is the key word. Parents may suggest or advise or even demand, but the freedom-conscious young American jealously guards his rights and insists on selecting the person he loves. There is much to be said for our system. But the climbing divorce rate surely proves that love can be blind, or at least fallible. How do I know I am in love? How do I know that this man or woman will be a good companion, will be a person I can spend the rest of my life with, will be a husband or wife who will make me happy and whom I can make happy? There is no simple answer, just as there are no easy solutions to life's real questions. But the more we know about love, about men and women, about individuals as persons, the better chance we have for a successful match.

It seems that the immature individual picks his sexual partner almost at random. In such a case, it often appears that as long as a man gets his woman and the female gets her male everything is under control. But in mature men and women, the process becomes more complicated. Ignace Lepp notes this fact:

> "As a general rule, however, it is true that the more mature an individual is and the more he functions as an independent person, the more complex his choice of a love-partner becomes. The Russian novelists of the nineteenth century even went so far as to maintain that there is only one woman in the world for any individual man, and only one man in the world for any one woman. They were 'destined for each other from all eternity.' This undoubtedly would limit in the extreme the chance for a happy choice."[1]

It is not, as Lepp observes, that for the more mature person good looks cease to have any role in selecting a partner and falling in love. It is more a question that other factors enter the picture and tend to replace physical attractiveness as the decisive motive for love. Chance also plays a great part. How frequently a man and woman who grew up together, who were neighbors and classmates, but never lovers, suddenly "discover" each other, fall in love and eventually marry. Something at that time put one or both of them in a frame of mind where they were more receptive to love entering their lives.

I think Lepp well summarizes the overall complexity of this phenomenon:

> "It is useless — in the majority of cases, at least — to try to explain the birth of love in

terms of a single driving force. Generally it is a whole ensemble of causes and a set of extremely complex motivations that serve to ignite the fire of love. Physical and psychological factors are inextricably intertwined, with the predominance of one set of factors at one time and of the other set at another time, even in the same individual. And since unconscious motivations seem to outweigh by far the conscious motive of an individual, the subject himself is almost never in a position to tell us why he loves one particular person. As a rule, it is only in the course of depth analysis that the real explanations of his love are disclosed, and often to the great astonishment of the person concerned."[2]

The priest-psychiatrist also observes something else that contains value for the present discussion:

"It rarely happens (except in certain Russian novels) that an individual falls in love only once in his lifetime. It is a fact that the same individual is capable of choosing a succession of partners on the basis of conscious and unconscious motives that are different every time. The more a person becomes a distinct individual the more complex the human psyche."[3]

His observations can be somewhat disconcerting for the young person or couple in love. For him, her or both love is unique, eternal, exclusive. I often hear from a brokenhearted lover that he or she will never love again, will never be able to love another person, that no other love will be the same. Part of this lament, of course, is true; but time mends many hearts and later the same individual finds it possible to develop a wonderful, though different, love relationship with some other person. These comments carry special force in our days for the aged, the adolescent, and for the engaged girl whose fiancé has been suddenly killed in military action or by accident.

As we list the complex and multifaceted motives for love, the element of chance, the possibility of falling in love several times during life, it may seem futile to attempt to make responsible choices about love and a future partner. This is not the case. "Falling in love," as we will see in the next chapter, particularly for the first time, can be essentially a blind, emotional, unrealistic experience, however beautiful and valuable. But "standing or staying in love" is something else. So, too, is selecting a partner with whom you will live, hopefully, for the rest of your days on earth. The more we know about a particular person, the better we understand his moods, his traits, his ups, his downs, the longer we grow "accustomed to his face," the greater the possibility that our relationship is a deep, lasting love, a love which will endure "until death do us part," and beyond.

To help sharpen the reader's critical judgment and to assist him or her in evaluating a person, I offer some positive qualities that should be present in a prospective partner. Then I will sketch a few negative characteristics which ideally ought not be present in a future companion.

Positive Qualities

A few years ago some students in a college listed several qualities they hoped to find in their future wives. I use this summary as a starting point to facilitate some sort of orderly treatment of the subject. The qualities are not placed necessarily in any order of importance. However, good looks were and are *not* first in their or my consideration.

1. *Compatibility*. Fundamentally this means an ability to live happily together. It demands a basic similarity in tastes, interests, social class, race, religious interests, age. Still, as in the matter of psychological traits in men and women, so here there can be and often is a complicated blending of likes and dislikes, similarities and differences in two lovers and two marriage partners. A disparity in age or race or social class, for example, does not automatically rule out a happy union. But it does of necessity demand a greater adjustment upon the part of each person involved, a greater maturity, a greater flexibility in accepting some root differences between one another.

The lover of Beethoven may grow weary of the partner who listens only to the Beatles; the regular reader of the Sunday *New York Times* may become discontented with the other member of the marriage who never passes beyond the comics or the sports.

In our rapidly integrating United States the question of interracial marriages must be faced. As schools and plants and neighborhoods see people of different races mingling freely and easily, it is only a matter of time until a racial mingling in matrimony will come. Those who are pioneers in this surely will suffer. I have worked enough in inner-city areas to know that often the persons joined in such a marriage tend to be rejected by both races. My advice to the young adults who have come to me in the past is only a word of caution. I see nothing in God's plan forbidding such unions. But the social pressures of contemporary society must be realistically reckoned with and hence I would sketch for the couple some of the obstacles they must overcome to enjoy a happy life together.

A variation in religious attitudes should be considered. Later I will treat as a separate unit the question of mixed marriages, i.e., a union between two persons of different faiths. The matter of religious attitudes refers, instead, to a basic feeling or trait. Some people seem deeply religious and concerned about church and Sunday worship and activities related to God and religion. The partner who shows little concern for such spiritual things presents an adjustment challenge to the other deeply religious person.

So, too, a considerable gap in social class or family background can spell trouble for the prospective husband or wife. Charity covers a multitude of sins and love, it seems to the young couple, obliterates all barriers. But the harsh realities of daily living impose burdens that not even the strongest love can overcome. The wealthy girl acclimated to luxuries of every sort may discover that frugal early years in marriage can be extremely trying.

It is a fascinating question to speculate on the reasons behind a successful love relationship. Is it because two persons share so many things in common? Or is it because they are different and complement each other? Later I will talk a bit more on this question. Here I think it should be noted that if there are real differences in the areas described above, the couple must recognize the necessity for greater adjustments in their relationship. Otherwise, excessive tensions will develop and bring about the death of their love.

2. *Education and intelligence.* In some ways this could be related to compatibility and the points on differences I have just covered. The college graduate may later on in marriage find it difficult to converse in a satisfying manner with a partner whose formal education stopped at the high school level. Nevertheless, the fact that an individual graduated from an institution of higher learning does not insure intelligence or an intelligent approach to life. Education refers in my view to formal, scholastic training; intelligence denotes an attitude, an ability to think, to be concerned about the serious issues of life and the world today.

Some time ago I led a small group of Central New Yorkers on a tour of Europe. One day in Copenhagen, Denmark, I was visiting with the manager of the hotel in which we were staying. A group of American college students, mostly girls, suddenly stormed into the lobby with their luggage. They, too, were touring and wished to check in for a few days' visit in this beautiful city. I asked the manager his opinion of the American girl. He said he was singularly unimpressed. During the course of a summer large numbers of the college set from the United States stay at his hotel. Their interests, in his view, were limited to candy, cigarettes and cute gifts for one another. They were all educated young women, but he felt they were not intelligent persons — they seemed to have neither time nor interest in higher, more serious matters, in thinking, discussing, philosophizing. I am not about to agree with his observation, but the incident proves one point — to be educated does not necessarily mean you are intelligent, a profound thinker, and interested in the fundamental issues of life.

It has been suggested that, if there is a difference in intelligence or in education particularly, then the male should possess the better training and be the more intelligent. This, it seems to me, is based on the notion that the man must or needs to feel superior and, if his wife is in fact better educated and enjoys a keener mind, he will be unhappy and discontented. As a practical rule based on our contemporary society and the prevailing "male mystique," perhaps the suggestion contains some merit. One can question, however, its deeper, intrinsic value.

What seems of more importance for a happy mutual relationship is the ability to communicate and discuss. Normally such conversation and honest communication is easier for a couple if their educational backgrounds are similar and their thinking abilities run roughly parallel. But there are frequent exceptions to this norm.

3. *Good health.* Posters urge us: "Hire the handicapped." It could be argued, therefore, that to marry the handicapped would be an equally noble act. In such an instance I might praise the person's nobility, but I am not certain I could promise individual happiness in marriage. All too many young women marry out of sympathy, to help the unfortunate, to reform the sinner. The union, of course, can be successful and happy, but it will demand patience and adjustments of a heroic degree.

The young man who has lost a good portion of one arm in a childhood accident and whose intellectual capabilities do not fit him for a clerical position will find it difficult to obtain a position of employment with a high salary scale. His future wife must recognize that fact when she accepts his proposal. The prospective wife, nervous and anxious and with a family background of mental illness, may, in later years, slip into similar moods of deep depression and anxiety. Her partner must honestly accept that possibility when he exchanges vows at the altar. He promises to take her for better or for worse. Does he truly understand what that can mean?

Recently I witnessed the nuptial promises of an older couple who had to overcome substantial problems before they could marry. Within a few weeks, before they had even unpacked and settled in their new apartment-home, the wife was hospitalized for treatment of a small cancer. The worry, dread and uncertainty which surrounds this disease flooded both of their hearts. As the husband sat and sought some support in his moment of anguish, the words of the ceremony seemed so clear: "In sickness and in health, until death do us part." Little did they expect that their love would be so severely tested in a matter of days.

I suppose the theme of this section and chapter is a plea to avoid dreamworlds. Life is mixed with joys and sorrows. Matrimony includes both of them. The person afflicted with poor health may love more and become the perfect partner in marriage. But the healthier companion must understand that sickness and handicaps can place unusual stress upon a mutual relationship. Those so joined in wedlock must love and adjust more than the average couple if their union is to be a lasting and happy one.

4. *Disposition.* Disposition means a general attitude of mind and feeling. Persons are jovial, morbid, moody, enthusiastic, serious, agreeable, unpleasant, flighty. The person in love should try to evaluate his own disposition and that of his beloved. It is not easy. Nor is it possible to state what is the most successful combination of temperaments. I know married couples who seem to be of like dispositions. The quiet, serious, devout girl marries a retiring, conscientious, religious boy. But then I know couples who appear to have contrasting temperaments. The outgoing, aggressive man marries a shy and submissive woman. She is quite content being protected by him and offering him the adulation and affection he needs. It is confusing to say the least.

Lepp states: "In love, the individual seeks and hopes for his own realization in another person. From the earliest age, an ego-ideal begins to take shape in the psyche of an individual. The ego-ideal never ceases to look for its own realization in all the vicissitudes of life."[4] A physician-friend of mine thinks that a man seeks to find his fulfillment and complement in his wife and vice versa. This seems to be another way of stating what Lepp maintains. Thus the aggressive husband may find his complement in the affectionate and dependent wife.

The controversy makes for interesting discussion, especially for the couple trying to analyze their own relationship. I do not think it is tremendously important to know whether you as a couple are a blend of likes or opposites. However, I do think it is essential for each member of a couple to understand the other's disposition and temperament. Severe differences, again, mean greater adjustments in marriage. Similarities reduce some of that. In addition, it is vital for each to remember that the general tendency is to put one's best foot forward on a date, in the company of the beloved. A more accurate picture of his or her real temperament can be seen in the casual, relaxed atmosphere at home with the family or with close friends. The true disposition of a man or woman reveals itself better in these customary surroundings than in the artificial and sometimes charged situation of a dinner, dance or drive-in.

5. *Home loving.* Recently a young girl tearfully telephoned me to announce the cancellation of her upcoming wedding. Shortly thereafter her former fiancé came in to explain the change in plans. It turned out that he was the one who suddenly hesitated at the thought of marriage and sought at least a postponement of the wedding. He still loved the girl, dated her, and indicated little interest in anyone else. But the thought of making that final decision, of a permanent commitment to the responsibilities of marriage and family life overwhelmed him. He did not feel ready to settle down.

A woman generally expects that her new husband will be, basically, a home-lover. She wants him to like children, to enjoy staying at home in the evenings with her, to be responsible about domestic duties as well as office obligations. She does not normally resent an occasional or weekly night out with the boys, but she does grow troubled and anxious if his outings are frequent and lengthy.

The man has similar expectations about his future wife. The old adage about reaching a man's heart through his stomach contains more than a shred of truth even in today's world of packaged dinners. The girl who can cook, who is neat, who maintains a warm, pleasant home, stands a far better chance of holding the interest and love of her husband than the woman who is careless about these things. The weary and tension-filled man who returns to a sloppy house, a messy wife, several totally undisciplined children and an ill-conceived and poorly prepared dinner will be sorely tempted to look for release from his weariness and worries in other places and from other people— the bar, the boys or some sympathetic blonde.

It is a wise young lady who early learns from the future mother-in-law those dishes her fiancé especially enjoys.

6. *Good looks.* I have observed earlier that the more mature a person becomes the more complex are the motives which enter into his selection of a partner and life companion. The immature person generally does not pierce the surface of good looks and physical appearance. Our own sex-obsessed culture (we sell nearly every product with a pretty girl or a handsome man attached to it) fosters the attitude of choosing on the basis of bodily attractiveness alone. However, the Miss America winner does not *automatically* qualify as a satisfactory love-partner or future wife and mother. She may be. But the man who marries her does so because he has discovered what she is like as a total person, as a real woman; he has not been captivated by her physical, superficial beauty alone.

Nevertheless, beauty and good looks do play their part. It is not wrong for a man to be proud of his beautiful wife or a woman to cherish her handsome husband.

7. *Religion.* I refer here, as mentioned earlier, to a partner's specific religious faith and not to his or her religious attitude and disposition. For Americans the major divisions today probably are Protestant, Catholic, Jew and nonbeliever. A marriage between two Catholics, two Protestants, two Jews, two nonbelievers is not by that fact determined to be a successful one. Nor is a mixed marriage, i.e., between two individuals of different faiths, necessarily destined for disaster. But as I have noted in other areas, major differences demand greater adjustments on the part of the persons involved.

Nancy Clutter, one of the members of that Kansas family murdered in cold blood, had been steadily dating for several years the local high school basketball hero, Bobby Rupp. On the night of the fatal shooting they had returned rather late from a date and her father had some plain things to say to Nancy, statements "that concerned less the lateness of the hour than the youngster who had driven her home." Truman Capote continues the story:

"Mr. Clutter liked Bobby, and considered him, for a boy his age, which was seventeen, most dependable and gentlemanly; however, in the three years she had been permitted 'dates,' Nancy, popular and pretty as she was, had never gone out with anyone else, and while Mr. Clutter understood that it was the present national adolescent custom to form couples, to 'go steady' and wear 'engagement rings,' he disapproved, particularly since he had not long ago, by accident, surprised his daughter and the Rupp boy kissing. He had then suggested that Nancy discontinue 'seeing so much of Bobby,' advising her that a slow retreat now would hurt less than an abrupt severance later—for, as he reminded her, it was a parting that must eventually take place. The Rupp family were Roman Catholics, the Clutters, Methodist—a fact that should in itself be sufficient to terminate whatever fancies she and this boy might have of some day marrying."[5]

The thorny challenge of a mixed marriage is not limited to Catholic-Protestant situations like the Clutter case. Leslie Rawlings, as the daughter of a Congregationalist minister, knew the problems before her when she sensed a growing affection and a beginning love for Rabbi Michael Kind. In a pluralistic society like that of the United States, mixed marriages are here to stay, at least as far as my experience and statistics indicate. During 1964, for example, in our own parish church, over half of the 70 weddings performed were mixed marriages. In that same year, seven of the first ten nuptial services at which I officiated were mixed ones. These are facts we must face.

I speak about mixed marriages from personal experience and not from any position as a distantly removed Roman Catholic priest. My parents and grandparents both were involved in mixed marriages. One side of my family was Roman Catholic; the other, Episcopalian. I have lived in this kind of situation for nearly 40 years. My first 18 years were spent in neighborhoods that were heavily Protestant and my precollege education was totally in areas without Roman Catholic schools. As a public school product, a graduate of Andover and a student at Yale, I was exposed to persons of many faiths. I could hardly be accused of coming from the "Catholic ghetto."

My own feeling about religiously mixed marriages based both on personal experience and work as a priest can be summarized in three simple principles:

a. *Two persons can be happy in a mixed marriage.* This is an obvious truth but it needs to be stated. The testimony of many couples, my own parents included, confirms the possibility of deep happiness and love even when there is a difference on an issue so vital as one's relationship to God.

b. *A mixed marriage is not a perfect marriage.* One can rightfully ask if any marriage is a perfect or ideal one. Nevertheless, the fact remains that in a mixed marriage there exists a constant source of some division and lack of unity. This, of course, can be minimized and the emphasis placed on elements which unify (something attempted in a small pamphlet called *Making the Most of Mixed Marriages*). Yet husband and wife, with religious differences, simply will not be of one mind and heart in all ways.

c. *In a mixed marriage there are some added dangers for a successful marriage.* These are not insuperable dangers, but they must be dealt with in a realistic manner. How are the children going to be raised? In his Church, or hers, or neither? Are husband and wife going to his Church, or her Church, or separately, or to no Church? Are the husband and wife and, later, the children, going to pray together? If so, how, in what way? Does one partner accept divorce as a permitted alternative, if the marriage runs into rough water, and does the other partner not? The list of questions could go on. These are painful problems and admit of no facile solutions. The young man and woman should realize what adjustments a mixed marriage demands and strive to resolve as many of them beforehand as possible.

The one absolutely certain advice I have for young Americans dating in a country wonderful in its mixture of races and religions: Before you fall deeply in love with another person, find out what are his or her religious beliefs. If the chasm separating you is so deep that no amount of adjusting and discussing will bridge it, then it is far better to break up before your hearts become so intertwined that separation can be brought about only at a fearful price of excruciating pain and tears.

Negative Qualities

The presence of many positive qualities in a partner offers some encouragement that a life together with him or her could be successful and happy. The presence of one of many of the following negative traits, on the other hand, should serve as a warning. It should force the young lover to think twice, to wonder seriously, whether or not a person with such a weakness or bad characteristic could be a good partner forever.

It should be kept in mind that some traits which seem so desirable before marriage may not be equally attractive afterward. The young woman may relish traveling with a fast-spending, freewheeling, always moving, eagerly sought young man. Later, in the silent and long hours of an evening alone in the apartment, she may not so treasure those qualities. As he continues in married life to roam and spend and seek excitement, she may regret not having married a more stable, home-loving individual. The young man may rejoice in courting a beautiful and elegantly dressed girl, a socialite who gladly joins him for every party, every movie, every dance. Later, when he discovers she shows no interest in cooking food or cleaning house, his thoughts about her desirable qualities may change.

1. *Selfishness.* Since love essentially means self-giving, the selfish person actually lacks in love. It is not terribly difficult to discover this before marriage. The partner in courtship may not be selfish to his companion, but how is his relationship to parents, brothers and sisters, friends, older people? Does he trample on them, insist on his own way, dominate them, have a temper tantrum when he does not get what he wants? Can he laugh at himself and accept disappointments without bitterness? Is his heart closed to other people? Is he wrapped up in his own world, in his own problems? Does he really listen to others? Is he jealous, critical of others? Does he rarely speak well about anyone else? The questions, of course, apply with equal vigor to the girl. "She" can be substituted for "he" in each one.

We must not dream an impossible dream about the partner we love. Only God is perfect. We all have faults. Everyone constantly struggles or should struggle to overcome selfish tendencies. But some are more selfish than others and less inclined to work against this particular tendency. The person whose partner manifests unusually frequent and severe selfishness should think deeply before accepting that kind of companion for life.

2. *Immaturity.* Maturity means flexibility, an ease in adjusting, a general control of our feelings. The emotionally immature man or woman remains a little child. This kind of person is easily hurt, quick to anger, slow to forgive, inclined to pout. Stubborn, unbending, overly critical, such an individual also goes to pieces about little things. The bothersome antics and foibles of children annoy this immature person.

Fortunately, the immature can grow up and out of their childish attitudes and behavior. But a good start along the road should be in evidence before the vows and rings are exchanged at the altar. Otherwise, it may mean a permanent baby-sitting job for the more adult partner.

3. *Drunkenness and infidelity.* It is an old saying

that first comes Punch, then comes Judy. Often in a person and in a marriage, drink and sex seem closely related. It is not uncommon for a person to start out in a bar and end up in a bed. Heavy drinking before marriage by one partner, to the usual distress of the other, should be a clear emergency danger signal. Generally the situation does not improve after the wedding; it worsens. After all, before marriage the man is trying to win the favor of his girl and the woman is seeking to attract the man she loves. Each one tends to be on a best behavior basis. Later, after vows, the individuals are inclined to return to their more honest and real selves. How dreadful an error for one to marry a prospective alcoholic with the hope of reforming that kind of person. It seldom, if ever, happens—much to the misery and later grief of the injured party. We need to love the sinner and the weak; but charity begins at home when evaluating marriage partners.

Unfaithfulness raises its ugly and disastrous head in courtship when one partner discovers his or her promised spouse is dating others during engagement. If fidelity is impossible under the best premarital circumstances, then how can anyone possibly hope for faithfulness to one bed, one partner, one home, one family during the more humdrum days of marriage? The absence of strong religious convictions and courage, as well as a code of vague and irresponsible morality, does not augur well for marital fidelity. As Ignace Lepp says: "Husbands and wives require solid moral principles and great strength of character in order to resist and overcome the erotic attraction they will inevitably experience for another woman or another man when habit will have succeeded in dulling the erotic charm of their married life."[6]

The fictional Michael Kind at 15 was sadly shocked one winter evening when he unexpectedly discovered an example of this marital infidelity in his own family. He had been doing some research for a term paper in biology on the massive reproductivity of Trypetidae, the family of which the fruit fly was a member. On his way home from the library at New York University and heavily burdened with books, he noticed the light burning in his father's office. Delighted at the prospect of traveling home in comfort on a cold, drizzling evening instead of facing a long, standing subway ride, he climbed the four flights of stairs and opened the door to Kind Foundations. There in front of him, his father was making love to the firm's secretary, Carla Salva, on the worn couch he vacuum-cleaned so industriously every Saturday morning. Carla lazily opened her eyes, looked straight at Michael, and screamed.

He turned and crashed down the dark hallway to the stairs. "Who was that?" he heard his father's voice demand.

And then: "Oh, my God."

He was on the second floor landing when Abe began to shout down the stairwell. "Mike. Mike, I've got to talk to you."

He continued to crash down the stairs until he was out of the building and into the icy rain. Then he ran. He sprawled on the ice as a taxi horn blared and a driver cursed him in Southern tones, and he got to his feet and began running again, leaving his books and his notes where they had fallen.

When he reached 34th Street he was sick and out of breath and he stumbled toward the subway steps.

He didn't remember how he got home. But he knew that he was in bed. His throat felt as though it had been rubbed with a potato grater, his head throbbed, and he burned. He felt like a bunsen burner; when they turn me off, he thought, nothing will be left but the container.

Sometimes he dreamed of Carla, of her open mouth, slack and wet, and of the thin nostrils dilating in passion like the slow motion of butterfly wings. He was conscious that he had imagined her that way recently, and he was ashamed.

Sometimes he dreamed of the fruit fly, reproducing with magnificent ease, gaining far more efficiency out of the mating procedure than man, but no ecstasy, poor thing.

Sometimes he heard a drum, beating up into his ear through his hot pillow.

Two days after he became ill he came to his senses. His father was sitting on a chair next to the bed. Abe was unshaven and his hair wasn't combed.

"How do you feel?"

"All right," Michael said hoarsely. He remembered everything as if the scenes were sculpted in blocks of crystal and set before him in a row.

Abe looked at the door and wet his lips with his tongue. In the kitchen Michael could hear his mother doing the dinner dishes.

"There are lots of things you don't understand, Michael."

"Go play with your weights."

The hoarseness made him sound on the verge of tears. The fact that this was so filled him with rage. What he felt was not sorrow but icy hate, and he wanted his father to know.

"You're a kid. You're a kid, and you shouldn't judge. I've been a good father and a good husband. But I'm human."

His head hurt and his mouth was dry. "Don't you every try to tell me what to do," he said. "Never again."

His father leaned forward and looked at him piercingly. "Some day you'll know. When you've been married twenty years."

They could hear his mother put down her dish and start toward his bedroom. "Abe?" she called. "Abe, he's up? How is he?" She came hurrying into the room, a fat woman with sagging breasts and thick ankles and ridiculous red hair. Just to look at her made everything worse.

He turned his face to the wall.[7]

This kind of unpleasantness, of course, can happen in marriage. The possibility of its occurrence, however, is much less when the premarital history shows a strong fidelity to each other, and deep religious and moral convictions.

It is generally a delusion to hope for some profound conversion *after* marriage. If there is to be one, as I mentioned in the preceding chapter, it normally comes before the wedding day.

4. *Irresponsibility.* A wife needs security in her home. The husband who flits from job to job offers precious little of that. To depend on welfare, to live hand to mouth, to have nothing aside for "a rainy day," to wonder and worry about tomorrow's food and the next semester's clothes is hardly the kind of life a woman wants. But a boyfriend who spends money like it is going out of style, who saves little, who grows restless with his work after a short period of time, who seems unconcerned about training for a better future in our increasingly automated age, who manifests little sense of responsibility—that kind of boyfriend very likely will become the irresponsible husband.

So, too, although in a less obvious manner, the young woman who buys foolishly, who neglects duties around her family home, who cannot be depended upon at work, who seems to show no interest beyond fun and games—that kind of irresponsible person easily can become a wife who abandons the children, grows careless in her housekeeping, spends a husband's pay check without thought or concern, and ends up seeking escape from dry and dull duties at home by searching for exciting people and places outside the house.

5. *Religious indifference.* The person who rarely attends church, seldom prays, manifests little interest in religion before marriage, probably will show less afterward. A husband or wife hardly enjoys attending church alone. This, in itself, can be a serious drawback in a mixed marriage. But when one of the partners practically ignores God, the other, if seriously concerned about religious values, not only will end up going to church alone but will also find this lack of sharing in religion a heavy burden to bear. The man or woman may push and pull and struggle to get the other out of bed Sunday after Sunday. But eventually he or she tires of fighting and regretfully ends up by going to church alone. Is this what the young man or woman wants out of marriage? It is a good question

to ask during the time of serious courtship.

6. *No desire for children.* I have found few men or women who felt this way before marriage. What might be noticed is an unfortunate harshness toward children that could spell trouble later on in marriage. The man who outwardly admits a desire for children of his own may betray a different inward attitude by his actions. If he has little time for them before marriage, if he is harsh, impatient, severe with them, then we can legitimately wonder if he will not be that way as a father. The same may be said of the woman.

It is wise, also, for the couple before marriage to talk about how they are going to raise their children, and what they will do if they discover that they are physically unable to have children. My experience, however, indicates that all or at least the huge majority of couples spend hours discussing their future life together, their children and all the other matters related to a home and a family. They normally need little urging to do so.

How To Be Sure

Max Kind asked his rabbi-father the question, "How do you know when you really love a girl?"

I find nearly every young adult is asking, at least silently, the same thing. How can I be sure? How do I know this is the real thing, the right person? How do I know I will be happy for life with this particular individual? How can we tell we are really in love?

The rabbi, after admitting he had no workable definition of love, advised his adolescent son in this way: "When the time comes, when you're older and you meet a woman you want to spend the rest of your life with, you won't have to ask."

There is some truth to this. As a many-splendored and mysterious thing, the love between a man and a woman sometimes starts strangely. Its growth or decline follows no rigid rules. Often the lovers know they are in love, but hardly can explain why or how.

Nevertheless, I feel that in sophisticated modern America the majority of persons need to make a decision about love which has some sort of reasonable basis to it. The essential harm of so many past motion-picture portraits was just this—the dreamy, unrealistic, instant love concept given to the audience. These things do happen and the couple occasionally does live happily ever after. But they are exceptions to the normal pattern. The more we know about love, about men and women, about the particular partner before us, the better prospect there is that the relationship of love is not surface, not ephemeral, but deep and permanent.

These first three chapters, I hope, supply the concerned couple with ample background ideas and information for making some kind of a reasonable decision about their relationship. However, as a further aid and a simpler one at that, I offer these five questions for the wondering young lover to ask himself or herself. A positive answer to all five does not guarantee the presence of love or insure matrimonial bliss, but it does indicate at least the beginnings of real love.

1. *Could we live happily together?* After we honestly examine ourselves, our good and bad qualities, our likes and dislikes, our similarities and differences, our backgrounds, our training, our hopes for the future, after we weigh the elements treated in this chapter and in the last one and apply them to ourselves—after we do all these things, does it seem we could live together with a minimal amount of tension and a maximum degree of harmony? Or are there just too many deep-seated clashes that eventually will explode and ruin the love we think now exists?

2. *Do I have a genuine reverence for the other partner?* Do I respect him, place him or her on a pedestal? The pedestal should not be elevated too high, divorced from human frailty and the harsh realities of daily life. But granted this reservation, is there the tendency to truly admire and revere my companion?

3. *Do I normally put my best foot forward in his or her presence?* As the courtship lengthens there will be a more relaxed, a more natural and open attitude between lovers. The real selves will tend to appear from beneath the artificial veneer offered in the beginning of the relationship. This, of course, is important and valuable. But is there always a desire that he or she see me at my best, not at my worst?

4. *Do I tend to reveal my inner self to her or to*

him? Many of us are afraid to love, to open our hearts to other people. The person who does love and who does open his heart exposes it to injury. We can be hurt. So human beings hide their true feelings until they trust another person. Then, little by little, depending upon the personality of the individual, the doors to the heart open wider and wider and we take our friend, our companion, our lover, our spouse more and more inside. As I have described, the "male mystique" that a man should hide his feelings and retain his "superiority" in such a way actually makes this question more pertinent. The man who may be crippled by this false male stereotype, who fiercely guards his inner self, and who begins to reveal those hidden hopes and fears, certainly manifests great trust and confidence in his newly discovered listener and confidant. In that kind of person, the tendency to reveal one's inner self is an excellent sign of love.

5. *Do I tend to be thoughtful, considerate, unselfish in his or her presence?* This follows from the root notion of love as self-giving. Am I quite happy simply making my partner happy? Very likely this question is the pivotal, absolutely essential one that must be answered in the affirmative. Unless it is, the love will surely die and the future marriage certainly will end in disaster.

I am not sure the boy should buy a ring or the girl call the church simply because they can answer "yes" to all five questions. But it gives some encouragement for them to have high hopes.

* * *

At the beginning of this book Tony asked Ann, "Don't you really love me?" He was, in effect, saying, "If you really love me, you will let me pet with you or even go all the way." Now I have not as yet supplied Ann with a full answer. But at least she and Tony may be able to decide a little better if they do love each other.

Unfortunately, looked at in one way, Tony is asking Ann to prove her love. The reader of these first three chapters must have arrived at least one incontrovertible conclusion: Love is very complex, and knowing you are in love is an even more complicated matter. To see petting and sexual intercourse as a proof of one's love is terribly simplistic. After all, you can pet and sleep with a prostitute and not love her. To demand these physical elements as a sign and proof of one's love complicates an already involved question.

I will maintain, in the next and following chapters, that necking, petting, intercourse, those things we usually call sex, should be an expression (not a proof) of love and a means of creating new life. I also hope to complete Ann's answer to Tony. Perhaps then she will be able to say to him, "I do love you, but I would rather not pet or go all the way now—for these reasons."

4. Love and Life

*P*uberty announces the beginning of a revolutionary period in a person's life. A time for change. A process of becoming. One rejects the thoughts, actions and feelings of a child and accepts the thoughts, actions and feelings of a man. Signs of childhood are gradually cast aside—a mother's breast, the sucking thumb, the blanket, the teddy bear, the warm and secure home, parents who love and care regardless of the child's behavior. In their stead, the adolescent little by little chooses the signs of manhood and womanhood—independence, freedom, personal responsibility, explanations, new friends and houses and places. It is a time to dream dreams, have high hopes, entertain visions of grandeur, a time to want to be a young man or a young woman, not a little boy or a little girl.

But like all revolutions, adolescence is neither serene nor static. True, it starts out serenely enough. Slow, small bodily and emotional changes pave the way. They ever so imperceptibly hint at the dawn of a new world, one of maturity and parenthood. But suddenly the whole picture is crashingly unveiled with the first menstruation or nocturnal emission. These may be traumatic experiences. Still, aware and informed parents can make such phenomena relatively painless, even joyous. Fathers and mothers who either don't care or don't understand can, by their omission, cause these new events to be painful and frightening. In any case, the young persons have to be somewhat disturbed. They have been given a glimpse of the picture. A fleeting one, but a glimpse. They cannot, even if they wish, put it out of their minds. Serenity, now, is not for them.

This particular revolution lasts a long time. It contains great victories and unfortunate defeats. There are small advances and temporary retreats. There are occasional leaps toward adulthood and maturity and some serious yearnings to return to the warmth of the womb. But the major part of the struggle is hard fought—some progress here, a setback there. Not all win the battle, nor do all equally succeed. Adjustment to this changing period in one's life varies with individuals and is based on an almost limitless number of factors. Ambivalence is the order of the day. The adolescent is dreamily confident, optimistic, exhilarated, a world conqueror. Away from this dreamworld, facing the harsh realities of life, he can be fearful, diffident, depressed, pessimistic. The young man or woman yearns anxiously for strength, maturity, firmness, self-understanding, self-control, self-acceptance. But those goals seem so distant, so vague that he frequently returns or at least desires to return to the protective arm of his father or would like to hide behind the serene and secure skirts of his mother. Yet, deep down, he understands, more and more so as he moves along, that such escape is cowardly and dooms one for total weakness and unhappiness. Growing up is hard.

Woven naturally and inextricably into the process of becoming a man or woman is sex. New powers and previously unknown desires arise in the adolescent. The boy becomes aware that girls are attractive and alluring. The girl realizes that boys are different and desirable. Since the urges are so new and physical and powerful and mysterious, the teen-ager tends to become fascinated with all of this, even obsessed with it. There is a great curiosity, a wonderment about one's self and about others. Sexual maturity and understanding, like fundamental self-acceptance, understanding and control, comes only after a long and more or less painful struggle. It, too, is neither serene nor static. Tears, grief, worry, heartbreak, shame—all may cloud the peaceful days of the teens and early twenties. And progress toward control and direction of the sexual drive generally is uneven and even unpredictable.

There are, of course, infinite variations in the way a young man or woman develops in the sexual area. We will describe a few of the more common ones.

Experimentation

Norman Vincent Peale once wrote that "Young people are going to experiment with sex: they always have and they always will. It's silly to pretend that they won't."[1] This is hardly surprising. I have just mentioned the adolescent's natural tendency to become obsessed, curious, facinated with his newly found powers and urges. For him or her to experiment with sex, alone or with others, is understandable enough. This is not to say, of course, that such exploratory activities are morally correct or that they are the best ways of growing into full maturity and manhood or that they will produce happiness in the heart. But it should give those of us charged with the guidance of youth—parent, educator, clergy—some sympathy for the situation.

Statistics confirm Dr. Peale's contentions. Marc Oraison, M.D., is a French priest and writer with more than ten years of specialization in modern psychology. In his very fine book, *Learning to Love,* he cites some pertinent statistical facts. Every serious study, Oraison notes, indicates that in contemporary society and under present conditions at least 95 percent of boys and young men between 13 and 25 years of age go through periods of habitual masturbation. The periods vary in length, sometimes lasting only for a few months, sometimes continuing for many years. Changing conditions in home or school do not seem to make significant differences in the incidence of masturbation. With girls, the situation is different. Only 40 to 50 percent actually pass through a period of such actual masturbation (with the genital parts). But they quite commonly resort to more indirect forms of self-excitation, such as having sentimental thrills, developing romantic "crushes" on certain boys, caressing the body.[2]

Experimentation in sex with another is something else again. This requires a willing partner and the destruction of certain barriers of reserve surrounding sexual activities. However, the famous Kinsey report surely proves that many persons have had some experiences with sex before marriage. Leslie Rawlings was one of them.

Several times already in this book I have introduced the name and person of Michael Kind. Michael, as has been parenthetically observed, is the central figure in Noah Gordon's widely read ("6 Months on the New York Times Bestseller List") and recent novel, *The*

Rabbi. The story of his life and of his loves is told in warm and clever flashback style. We follow this young Jewish boy from early childhood into his middle forties. After the rather normal uncertainties of college, Michael finally decides on the rabbinate as his call, completes the necessary preparation and becomes a rabbi. Following a short stint in Florida, he moves to Arkansas as a sort of missionary to the Jewish flock scattered throughout that state. It is rough work with few of the comforts to which Michael as a native New Yorker has grown accustomed. Leslie Rawlings, the daughter of a Congregational minister, comes to visit her college classmate whose parents are members of the rabbi's congregation. Michael is attracted to the girl and eventually, on a picnic, he kisses her.

"I'm very grateful to you," she said.

"What for?"

"I responded when you kissed me. I responded very strongly."

"Is that so unusual?"

"It is for me ever since I had an affair last summer," she said.

"Hey." He leaned forward so that she had to stop cutting his hair, "You don't want to be telling me about something like that."

She grabbed him by the hair and pulled his head back. "Yes, don't you see, I haven't been able to tell anybody, but this is so safe. This is practically made to order. You're a rabbi and I'm a . . . a *shickseh,* and we'll probably never see each other again. It's even better than if I were a Catholic telling it to a priest hidden behind a screen in a confessional, because I *know* the kind of person you are."

He shrugged and sat quietly while the scissors snipped and the hair fell on bare shoulders.

"It was with this Harvard boy I didn't even like. His name is Roger Phillipson, his mother went to school with my aunt, and to please them we went out a couple of times so we could both write home about it. I let him make love to me in his car, only once, just to see what it was like.

It was simply awful. Nothing. Since then I haven't enjoyed kissing a boy and I've never been able to feel passionate. I was very worried. But when you kissed me after I caught the fish I felt as passionate as anything."

He felt both flattered and extremely annoyed. "I'm glad," he said. They were both silent.

"You don't like me as much as you did before I told you that," she said.

"It isn't that. It's simply that you caused me to feel like something that made the right color on your litmus paper."

"I apologize," she said. "I've wanted to tell somebody about that ever since it happened. I grew so disgusted with myself afterwards, and so sorry that I had let my curiosity get the better of me."[3]

Leslie's experimentation with sex cost her dearly. Actually we first meet her in the book as a patient in the Woodborough State Hospital. She is 40, attractive, the wife of a Jewish rabbi. Her diagnosis: involutional melancholia. Twelve electroconvulsive treatments and Thorazine, later supplanted by Pyrrolazote, have helped her overcome mental and physical weariness, irritability, restlessness, and insomnia. The medical case history reveals the problem.

"Amnesia resulting from the treatment appears to be minimal. In interviews with her psychiatrist during the past week the patient has told the therapist that she recalls maintaining silence because of a disinclination to share with anyone her guilt arising from an estrangement with her father and from the supposition that she was an unfit wife and mother because of a premarital sexual experience while she was a college student more than two decades ago. Her husband was made aware of this experience before their marriage, and the patient does not remember being bothered by any further remorse — or even thinking about the incident — until several months ago. While she clearly recollects the recent advent of guilt feelings regarding the youthful sexual incident and the loss of her father's love, these feelings of guilt no longer plague her. The patient now appears calm and optimistic.

"She described her sexual relationship with her husband as a good one. Her menstrual cycle has been irregular for almost a year. Her present illness apparently is an anxious, agitated delusional depression of the menopause."[4]

I in no way wish to imply by this excerpt from *The Rabbi* that every person who experiments with sex alone or with someone else suffers guilt feelings and subsequent emotional difficulties. Leslie Rawlings' anxieties were both extreme and complicated by circumstances. Nevertheless, it is unquestionably true that many young people and older adults do experience remorse for some sexual experimentation similar to Leslie's.

Michael Kind will return later in this chapter.

First Love

A first kiss, first petting experience, even first premarital sexual intercourse is not necessarily identical with first love. They may or may not be linked. But the initial experience of "falling in love" can very well be one of the most pivotal, blind, thrilling, painful, wonderful events in a young person's life.

Twenty-five years ago, Maureen Daly wrote a novel, *Seventeenth Summer,* about Angie Morrow's first love — for a boy named Jack Duluth. Their romance lasted but a few months. It began and ended during the summer following her graduation from high school. The book would be judged naive and innocent by present-day standards. However, it captures well the pain and thrill of first love. How else can one explain that it has sold over 300,000 copies, that it has, apparently, been read by every high school girl even today, that as recently as 1966, a quarter of a century later, the publishers made their 42nd printing of it?

In the opening chapter, Angie describes what happened to her during that summer vacation when she was 17:

"I don't know just why I'm telling you all this. Maybe you'll think I'm being silly. But I'm not, really, because this is *important*. You see, it was different! It wasn't just because it was Jack and I either — it was something more than that. It wasn't as it's written in magazine stories or as in morning radio serials where the boy's family always tease him about liking a girl and he gets embarrassed and stutters. And it wasn't silly, like sometimes, when girls sit in school and write a fellow's name all over the margin of their papers. I never even wrote Jack's name at all till I sent him a postcard that weekend I went up to Minaqua. And it wasn't puppy love or infatuation or love at first sight or anything that people always talk about and laugh. Maybe you don't know just what I mean. I can't really explain it — it's so hard to put in words but — well, it was just something I'd never felt before. Something I'd never even known. People can't tell you about things like that, you have to find them out for yourself. That's why it is so important. It was something I'll always remember because I just couldn't forget — it's a thing like that."[5]

Adults, wise with experience and probably hardened by the years, can easily deride the kind of first love Angie experienced. But to label it "puppy love," to make fun of it, to throw cynically cold water on this warm, tender feeling is neither humanly considerate nor educationally sound. Those like myself who deal with the young must, it is true, lead affectionate adolescents beyond simple surface feelings, but to do so demands considerable tact and wisdom.

This first love can easily be blind. It is heavily bound up with affection. The young lover sees a wonderful person whose spirit is enclosed in a body. But the strong feelings for the other, not necessarily sexual at this point, can cause the first lover to lose sight of reality and visualize qualities in this girl or boy that in fact do not exist. They are more projections of what they want to see or know in the young partner than actual positive attributes possessed. In time the glow may go and truth appear through the diminishing affection. It is the task of those guiding youth to help them learn through usually bitter experience that the wonderful "crush" does not always last, that later unpleasant qualities of the boy or girl may appear and become clear to the other, that living together as husband and wife demands a stronger and deeper love than this emotional, physical attraction. Such direction requires extreme patience, delicacy and prudence.

While blind and divorced from reality, this first love still can be extremely beneficial to the young man or woman. It is not always selfish, as some maintain. On the contrary, the boy, for example, who comes home and tells his parents that he (at 15) is in love with a classmate may well be tremendously self-giving during this period. She is, obviously, the most wonderful, beautiful thing that ever existed. He thinks about her, watches her with adoring eyes, copies her tastes and habits, is lonely without her, talks for hours with her, is overjoyed at a smile, a word, a sign of her reciprocal love. No price is too great to pay to be with her. Rain, snow, miles mean nothing to the young lover. Temporary it may be, but likely for the first time in his life, he has completely gotten out of himself and is concerned about another and willing to suffer and sacrifice personally for someone else.

The pastoral experience of priests can testify to this. As Dr. Oraison points out in his book, often a young man with a habit of masturbation will quite suddenly stop this practice upon falling in love. The self-satisfying procedure seems out of place. He instead wants to get out of self and give to another. And without sexually involving his new love. At first he may not have the least thought of this. Later on, as an expression of his great feelings for her, he may wish to kiss, caress, pet with her. But even then he may grow uncomfortable with himself and regret that he took his first love down from the elevated pedestal. The same boy may have known beforehand rather deep and extensive sexual experiences with one or several girls. But these are now judged selfish. It was a case of using them, of merely substituting girls and petting for masturbation. The first love in some cases can change all that.

Sex For Kicks

Sex is fun, in a sense. It is a basic appetite. We grow hungry for food, find pleasure in eating, feel satisfied and contented when full. A parallel exists with sex. The pleasure, however, is much more intense. Little wonder that over the ages some have argued that it is perfectly normal and permissible to indulge in sexual activities simply for the pleasure or fun of it. Little wonder, too, that the adolescent, striving confusedly to learn and understand himself and establish his identity as a distinct, rich individual, living in a highly sensate culture, breathing in an atmosphere where sex is employed to sell practically all products, hearing sophisticated arguments that sexual activities are perfectly natural and normal in or outside of marriage, may fall.

Michael Kind did.

In high school, he necked with the girl next door, more for thrills and to pass the time away and because it was sort of expected, than for love. He almost lost his virginity with Ellen Trowbridge one summer at Cape Cod. He cared for her (" 'I may be in love,' he said. It was the first time he had ever said that to a girl.")[6] and his arduous efforts with her during summer vacation were a typical intermingling of honest affection, hot-blooded desire, and curiosity. Later, in college, with Edna Roth, a young widow, he gave what a person can only give once. ("He felt weightless and happy, relieved of the burden of innocence. 'Finally,' he said aloud.")[7] This was not love, but it was not completely unfeeling and casual sex either. That came soon. And with it an awakening.

Michael and Maury Silverstein picked up a couple of girls ("pigs," Maury called them) and went to Maury's parents' apartment, vacated by them for the weekend. The boys with their partners separated into different rooms. After "making love" with Michael, the girl called to her friend and they switched rooms.

The future rabbi was, at first, excited by this strange turn of events, but the coarseness of it all, the awareness that the girls had done this many times, in many places, with many men suddenly sickened him. He quickly dressed and left. Returning home, he showered (with much scrubbing, scalding water and quantities of soap), but was in no mood for sleep. Climbing to the roof of his apartment he sat down and philosophized.

> "He could taste spring in the wind. The sky was studded with stars and he held his head back and stared at them until the breeze made his eyes fill and the glowing white points of light circled and swam in his vision. There has to be more to it than that, he told himself. Maury had called the girls pigs, but if so he and Maury had been pigs, too. He swore that he would have no more sex until he fell in love. The stars were unusually bright. He smoked a cigarette and watched them, trying to imagine how they looked without the interfering lights of a city. What held them up there, he wondered, and then the automatic answers came; he remembered vaguely about mutual attractions: the force of gravity, Newton's First and Second Laws of Motion. But there were so many thousands, scattered at such vast distances, and so balanced, behaving so steadily, circling precisely in their orbits like the works of a giant, beautifully constructed clock. The laws in the textbooks weren't enough, there had to be something else, otherwise for him the beautiful complexity was meaningless and without passion, like loveless sex."[8]

Michael did succumb later, once, to loveless sex. But it was more a mute testimony to the weakness of man than a change of principle.

Playboy

Sex for kicks probably finds its best expression for contemporary man in Hugh Hefner and his *Playboy* philosophy. *Life* in its October 29, 1965, issue told the story of "An Empire Built on Sex." Amply illustrated with appropriate photographs, the article paints a fairly good portrait of the man and his ideas. Diana Lurie's comments point out some of the weaknesses attached to this philosophy.

"Hugh Hefner, in his magazine and in his philosophy, has set himself up as an oracle of all that is fine and good and clean in man's relationship with woman. And, he insists, unmarried sex is one of the finest, cleanest, best parts of it — as long as it is by mutual desire and consent and nobody gets hurt.

"That last is where the rub comes. Hefner talks a great deal about equality for everybody, including women. But the way it works out, in both his private life and his magazine, men are a lot more equal than women.

"In Hefnerland, a woman is simply another aspect of the status-symbol mania that is stamped all over *Playboy*. She is no more or less important than the sleekest sports car or most expensive bottle of Scotch. A woman becomes depersonalized, an object for man's pleasure, something to pour his drinks, inflate his ego and look gorgeous on his arm as he parades in front of his pals."[9]

Cynthia Maddox, a four-time *Playboy* cover girl, now the magazine's assistant cartoon editor, served as Hefner's personal "special girl" for a period of time. She, like Leslie Rawlings in *The Rabbi,* seemed to pay heavily for her casual relationship.

"Now, after abdicating the role of special girl, Cynthia is still too unsure of her capabilities to leave the security of *Playboy*. And besides, she needs her salary to pay the psychiatrist she began going to as her relationship with Hefner began tapering off.

" 'Sometimes — God, I don't feel like I have any identity of my own,' says Cynthia. Now, as Hugh Hefner's ex-girl and a *Playboy* cover girl, she finds many men looking on her as a sort of trophy. They regard her as the living, breathing embodiment of everything *Playboy* stands for — and treat her accordingly.

"Cynthia hates this. 'I would like someone who really notices me, really can respect me, really can remember things about me — some man who thinks about me when I'm away from him.' "[10]

* * * *

I maintain, in this book, the following philosophy of sex:

Negatively, I reject the casual, sex-for-kicks approach.

I reject the notion that complete sexual experimentation before marriage is necessary for personal growth and happiness.

Positively, I hold that sex is made by God, good, warm, beautiful, tender, sacred.

I hold that sex should be an expression of love and that to use it simply for one's pleasure is to render it selfish and even harmful for a person's growth toward maturity.

I hold that the use of sex bears an intimate connection with the awesome mystery and creation of life and should be reserved for the situation where that new life can best be conceived, develop and come into full being, i.e., in marriage.

* * * *

Let me amplify those statements.

First of all, by way of commentary on the negative propositions, the rejection of casual sex and experimentation pretty much follows from the material just presented.

Experimentation will always be a challenge and a difficulty for the growing young man and woman. In a subsequent chapter, I will discuss in detail the question of man's weakness and the adolescent's propensity to experiment. Here I simply maintain in theory that sexual experimentation (either through masturbation, petting, or premarital sexual intercourse), while understandable, is neither necessary nor even automatically the best way to reach emotional maturity. The claim that "everyone is doing it" needs to be realistically faced and I plan to do that later.

Casual sex seems, in my judgment, to reduce something very special and sacred to a common and ordinary means of personal pleasure. There is great danger here that both parties are merely using each other. The boy obviously obtains relief and satisfaction from an emotional and physical point of view. The girl also, perhaps less evidently, satisfies similar needs, particularly her desire to be loved and wanted and cared for. It appears to me that such activity fosters selfishness in both parties and thus does not contribute to self-controlling and directing, self-giving attitudes fundamental to real love. I feel it is poor preparation for the real love of marriage.

Love

More important than the negative rejection of current attitudes, however, is my positive endorsement of the beauty and dignity of sex. It is unfortunate that in so many religious circles, including Catholic ones, approaches to sex in the past have been largely negative ones, more or less tolerating it as a necessary evil. There is little foundation for this in Sacred Scripture. After creating man to his own image and likeness, "God blessed them, and God said to them, 'Be fruitful and multiply, and fill the earth and subdue it.' . . . And God saw everything that he had made, and behold, it was very good" (Gen. 1:27-31).[11] Since God tells us, then, that sex is good we should look for reasons why—beyond the bald fact that it came from the creative hand of the Lord. That it magnificently expresses in an external, visible fashion one's inner love for another person is a very strong reason sex is good.

A lover wants to be at one, united with his beloved. Joy comes from being together, sadness at separation for young (or old) lovers. Recently I received an emergency telephone call at 6:45 a.m. A son with troubled voice asked for a priest to come and administer the last rites to his father. The older man in his seventies had gotten out of bed, then slumped into an adjacent chair and slipped into unconsciousness. I quickly drove to their home and ascended the stairs to the second-floor apartment. It was too late. The doctor was about to leave. With black bag in hand, coat over his arm and wearing a strained expression on his face, he quietly told me that the old man was gone.

His wife sat weeping softly on the bed next to her ashen and still husband. She caressed his face, as if trying to restore life where life was no more. She picked up his arm and held his hand, squeezing it without any response. Let go, the arm fell limply to his side. She groaned and half threw up her arms, realizing little by little that her companion for 53 years had left her. With despairing tears she spoke to her dead husband and wept, "You won't be with me anymore."

Such sadness at death's final parting serves to emphasize the joy and happiness in the union of this loving husband and wife.

But lovers not only want to be one, they also wish to give to one another. Even the teen-age boy with his "puppy love," as we observed, wants to give to his new love. Flowers, candy, attention, carrying her books, notes, the movies — all are gifts signifying the inner spirit of love and self-giving in his heart. Such sentiments are intensified a hundredfold for the engaged couple, and for the man and woman united in marriage.

Is there any union closer than that which exists between husband and wife in sexual intercourse? "Therefore, a man leaves his father and his mother and cleaves to his wife, and they become one flesh" (Gen. 2:24).[12] Perhaps there is, but no one can deny that sexual union enables a man and a woman to enjoy a closeness that expresses, deepens and supports their bond of love.

Sexual union likewise fulfills a couple's need for mutual self-giving. The man loans, we might say, his body to his wife; but he actually gives of himself, his seed of life. It is complete self-donation. He cannot retrieve this gift once given. The woman similarly loans herself, her body to him. She opens heart and body and accepts him and his gift. She responds, in true lovemaking. And, during an act of intercourse resulting in conception, she in addition, donates something of herself, the ovum. The fertilized ovum, the new life begun in her womb thus is neither his, nor hers, but theirs. There has been mutual self-giving bearing fruit in a child which will be a unique expression of their love.

Rollo May, in an excerpt from his forthcoming book, *Love and Will,* speaks about these values in sexual love:

> "Tenderness is a second value, a tenderness that is much more than indicated in that most unpoetic of all words, 'togetherness.' The experience of tenderness comes out of the fact that the two persons, longing as all individuals do to overcome the separateness and isolation to which we are all heir because we are individuals, can participate in a relationship that for the moment is not too isolated selves but a union. In this kind of sexual intercourse, the lover often does not know whether a particular sensation of delight is felt by him or by his loved one — and it doesn't make any difference anyway. . .
>
> "A final value inheres in the curious phenomenon in lovemaking: that to be able to give to the other person is essential to one's own full pleasure in the act. . . . But it is not sentimentality but a point which anyone can confirm in his own experience in the love act, that to give is essential to one's pleasure. . . . Just as giving is essential to one's own full pleasure, the ability to receive is necessary in the love interrelationship also. If you cannot receive, your giving will be a domination of the partner. Conversely, if you cannot give, your receiving will leave you empty."[13]

John O'Hara's writing may be pretty strong and realistic for some readers. But in his *Appointment in Samarra,* a brief episode movingly illustrates the possible beauty and fulfillment of sexual love. Julian English is a handsome socialite secure in his job and blessed with a beautiful wife, Caroline. The comfortable security of his work dissolves one day and he returns home tense, upset, torn with anger and despair. O'Hara tells the rest:

Caroline had her knees up under the bedclothes, with the magazine propped against her legs, but she was holding the cover and half of the magazine with ...er right hand.

She slowly closed the magazine and laid it on the floor. "Did you have a fight with him?" she said.

"He wouldn't see me." Julian lit a cigarette and walked over to the window. They were together and he knew it, but he felt like hell. She was wearing a black lace negligee that he and she called her whoring gown. Suddenly she was standing beside him, and as always he thought how much smaller she was in her bare feet. She put her arm inside his arm, and her arm gripped the muscle of the arm.

"It's all right," she said.

"No," he said, gently. "No, it isn't."

"No, it isn't," she said. "But let's not think of it now."

She moved her arm so that it went around his back under the shoulder blades, and her hand moved slowly down his back, along his ribs, his hips and buttocks. He looked at her, doing all the things he wanted her to do. Her reddish brown hair was still fixed for the day. She was not by any means a small girl; her nose rubbed under his chin, and he was six feet tall. She let her eyes get tender in a way she had, starting a smile and then seeming to postpone it. She stood in front of him and kissed him. Without taking her mouth away she pulled his tie out of his vest and unbuttoned his vest, and then she let him go. "Come on!" she said, and lay with her face down in the pillow, shutting out everything else until he was with her. It was the greatest single act of their married life. He knew it, and she knew it. It was the time she did not fail him.[14]

Here was great womanly fulfillment. Caroline, able to make her husband Julian feel important, needed, wanted, felt in return a sense of satisfaction. For as his wife she could be comfort in this sorrow, support in his failure, release from the tensions of work and life. This was love, mutual love, and the sexual action expressed it, deepened it, strengthened it.

A final example. Charlie W. Shedd is minister of the Memorial Drive Presbyterian Church in Houston, Texas. His daughter, Karen, after engagement, asked her father for some premarriage advice. He responded with a series of letters and later gathered them in a book entitled, *Letters to Karen,* with further subheading, "On Keeping Love in Marriage." He makes the point in an abstract, technical way which the dramatic incident from O'Hara's novel does in a concrete, practical manner.

> "You are a prudent wife when you look on sex, in part, as your opportunity to be a blessing to your husband. The tender women train themselves to receive a large measure of contentment just from contenting their men.
>
> "It is not true, in my counseling experience that both parties to the union *need* the same results every time. I have read some writers who say that a man must be able to bring his wife to climax on every occasion of sexual love. In my judgment there is just one thing wrong with this supposition — it simply isn't so.
>
> "Some women tell me that they love to minister to their husband's emotional needs even when they care nothing at all about physical culmination for themselves."[15]

Through these varied quotations and examples I have tried in this section to establish the fundamental principle that sex should be connected with love. It beautifully expresses love. It should, in my view, be judged something special, sacred, out of the ordinary. It should not, therefore, be used casually, treated lightly, or simply employed as reward for a dinner, or a movie, or a dance, or for anything else.

Life

In the award-winning film, *The Pawnbroker,* the cynical and broken Jewish storekeeper quotes Einstein. He says something to the effect that the greatest miracle in the world is the seed of life. It is not particularly important whether the quotation is accurate or not. The idea stands. And sex bears an intimate, necessary connection with this, possibly the greatest power of man — to cooperate in creating new human life.

An example from this writer's personal, family background illustrates the point. My older brother is a *cum laude* graduate in English from Harvard. He spent some 17 years as a writer, correspondent, journalist for the *Time-Life* concern. Because of his work, he has lived in many parts of the United States, in England and has traveled through several European countries. He has met and talked with numerous national and international figures. Presently as entertainment editor of the Los Angeles *Times,* he walks and talks and lives amidst the glory and glitter of the film world. Despite this rich background, he says the greatest moment of his life, the most moving experience he can recall, came soon after the birth of his first child. He is not given to pious platitudes. But he once remarked that when he looked through the glass window of the maternity ward and gazed upon his new son for the first time, he was absolutely shaken. "This is my son. Flesh of my flesh. He will look like me. How I behave now and in the future, how I train and raise him will influence his whole life. Here is a new person placed in my and our custody." Later reflection brought him to add another insight. This child was and is an ongoing, unique sign of the love existing between him and his wife. They alone could cooperate in producing this particular infant. No other combination could achieve this child. He forms even today a constant, living reminder of their mutual love which bore such wonderful fruit.

Traditional Catholic philosophic explanation of conception offers a theoretical base for the joyful moments experienced by father and mother in the course of pregnancy and birth. Simply explained, it sees conception of the child as a triangular effort. Man, woman, God cooperate in this joint venture. The male and female unite, physically, sexually, to produce the material of the new person. Granted the necessary fertilization of the ovum by the sperm, God enters the picture and by a direct, creative act contributes the spiritual, immaterial principle of life. We might say the parents give the body, God the soul. The child bears resemblances to mother and father in its physical, bodily being; it is made in God's image and likeness in the spiritual soul. While this oversimplifies a most mysterious process, it can bring home the awesome dignity of conception. An awareness of their part, of their association on a close, personal basis with God in continuing human life, should have certain obvious impact upon the thinking of parents. A similar understanding should cast an air of reverence around sex for the boy and girl, young man and woman, engaged couple. They one day hope to share in this work. They are, now, potential fathers and mothers.

Life comes to our aid again to concretize in a human, visual way, the lofty concepts just described. In the July 22, 1966, issue, Eleanor Graves wrote and Lennart Nilsson photographed a story called, "Unforgettable Moments of Pregnancy and Birth." In a previous article (*Life,* April 3, 1965) the same photographer revealed the profound beauty and miracle of human embryonic development in a prize-winning effort. However, the power of the later treatment rests in its ability to communicate the personal feelings of wife and mother, husband and father as they learned of the conception, lived through the pregnancy and experienced the birth of their first child. The inside title of the article gives a foretaste of what was to follow. "A Woman on Her Way to a Miracle." A supporting caption further described the story. "The long months and unforgettable moments of Margareta Falk's first pregnancy." I quote here and there from the text.

> "Whatever feelings pregnancy may arouse — delight, indifference, resignation, horror — the very idea of creating a new human being is awesome. Pregnancy is surely the most creative thing you will ever do — even if you have done it inadvertently. And the process itself is miraculous — so hard to believe that at an already appointed hour you will divide like some ancient cell, and suddenly it won't just be you any longer

but you and some other being, to whom you will be tied, by nerves and tissue and chemistry, all your life. This being is already within you, shouting in a sometimes deafening voice, look out, stand back, here comes a whole new person. And you are the lifeline, its substance, its nourishment. Only you can make sure that its bones are strong and its eyes are clear. How good you must be, how well behaved, how faithful to this being.

" 'We really weren't surprised, just very pleased with ourselves and with everything. . .'

" 'The first three or four months were terrible. I was tired and I felt slightly sick to my stomach all the time. . .'

"Understanding Margareta didn't always come easily to Willy. 'In the first month,' he says, 'Margareta changed so abruptly she was like a stranger. I did so much to help her around the house and we ate out so much that I couldn't believe she was as tired as she said she was. It didn't seem possible. She wanted to go to bed every night at 7:30. . .'

"At the beginning of the fourth month things abruptly got better. Willy's explanation is that Margareta at last understood and accepted her pregnancy, and that it was finally real. 'We were happy again, and when we made love, it was good, like it always had been. . .'

"In Margareta's fifth month one of the tremendous events of pregnancy took place — tremendous, but such a little happening that if she had not been on the lookout for it she might have missed it completely. 'One night as I was lying in bed,' says Margareta, 'I felt something, like bubbles, ginger ale. The baby moved. I was very surprised it was such a *little* feeling. I thought it would be much more, even at first. I told Willy and he put his hand on my stomach and we lay very still, but he couldn't feel it. . .'

"Once labor starts, you are on your way to a miracle and, after all, you have to live up to the occasion. . .

"All Willy could think of in the waiting room was now it would soon be over. 'I will get my wife back. Of course I will be a father too, but mostly I will have a wife again. It is very hard to be much of a couple toward the end of a pregnancy, and all I could think of was that we would be ourselves again. . .'

"It was 4:56. Richard Alexander Falk gave a wail. Willy looked him over carefully and concluded that his son looked just like him. Within two minutes Margareta regained consciousness and heard Willy calling, 'It's a boy, it's a boy. . .'

" 'At first I didn't know where I was and said, "What do you mean?" and then of course I knew completely, and I have never felt so happy before or after. My mother had told me that I would feel unbelievably good after the baby was born, but I didn't believe it would be anything like this. . .'

" 'I never get over how beautiful he is. Everytime I look at him I am surprised all over again,' says Margareta, lifting her 2-month-old son from his bassinet. 'I've forgotten pregnancy was ever hard.' "[16]

* * * *

The theme, in summary, of this chapter, as its title suggests, and of the entire book and our whole approach to sex and courtship and marriage is that sex embraces two profound elements—love and life. Loveless sex is out in such a view — it draws sex down from the lofty level where it belongs. Sex with love outside of marriage is also out in such a view — because the life which can flow from that kind of union needs a home, warmth, security, permanence, lasting care, attention. Weekend liaisons in motels or in the back seat of a car cannot offer those things.

5. *Why Wait Until*

*T*here are two burning questions asked constantly today by young adults. The first is: "Sex is natural and fun. What's wrong with enjoying it right now? Why wait?" The question is relatively easy to answer. In the last chapter I spoke about and rejected loveless or casual sex. Sex merely for fun and enjoyment is but a version of that philosophy. It fails for the same reasons that the sex-without-love notion fails.

The second question is: "If we are really in love and intend to get married sooner or later, then why isn't it perfectly legitimate for us to pet, make love, have intercourse? We are not adolescents. There is no question of being selfish. We are not using, deceiving or hurting each other. Eventually we may, why not now?"

This question is more difficult and vexing. The present chapter will look at this second question and attempt to offer some insights that may help persons concerned about it come to a good decision.

The words which follow, as might be expected, speak primarily to young men and women who are truly in love. They feel that they do share a sound and self-giving love. They may be engaged. But they may not be. After all, the presence of a sparkling diamond on a young lady's third finger, left hand does not automatically indicate the existence of a true, mature, lasting love between two people. Some girls receive their rings prematurely. Others are at this moment on the brink of returning them to the givers. On the other hand, many couples have already established a deep mutual love which augurs well for the kind needed in a lifelong union in marriage and yet have not, for a variety of reasons, publicized this fact to the world around them by means of engagement rings. This chapter addresses itself to couples, engaged or not, who are truly in love, deeply committed to one another and seriously planning a future marriage.

The question under consideration is not an academic one. Every rabbi, minister, priest, every teacher and

Marriage?

counselor, every person, in fact, who deals with young adults faces it frequently, even daily. Are engaged couples, or couples with the kind of mature love we mentioned, allowed extra liberties not granted to others? The question, however, is essentially a temporary one. I doubt if married people recall very often the sexual turbulence of courtship and the anxieties they felt then. Life moves on and new challenges occupy their attention and energy. But for the months or years immediately prior to the wedding it does, in many instances, toss the young lovers alternately up and down the emotional heights and depths. They feel a succession of bewildering emotions: elation, depression, guilt, anxiety, tension, peace. We should not exaggerate the problem; yet these anxious persons deserve some frank and positive assistance in charting a course to marital happiness.

Causes for Confusion

It is hardly surprising that modern-day couples are slightly confused. Talk about free love, unmarried love, premarital sex runs rampant. The young woman at 23 who still retains her virginity is told bluntly by a date that she is psychologically a misfit. He, of course, volunteers to initiate her into sexual maturity and aid her personal emotional growth. *Redbook* magazine runs a young mother's story. "Why I Believe in Sex Before Marriage."[1] College surveys chart graphs of attitudes in students showing that the majority favor a greater degree of permissiveness about sexual matters. Professors toss out remarks to the effect that chastity in courtship, virginity, "waiting until we marry," are basically medieval concepts based on erroneous notions of sex and love which have been perpetuated by frustrated celibate theologians. Commonly heard remarks are: "Everyone is doing it. That many Americans can't be wrong. Kinsey's statistics prove it." And so on, and on.

Anne Welles, the refugee from Lawrenceville in *Valley of the Dolls,* felt this kind of cultural pressure.

In New York City she found a job she liked, a girl-friend in Neely and a gentle, eager escort named Allen Cooper. Her boyfriend turned out to be a disguised millionaire, but despite his earnest efforts at courting Anne, she simply could not fall in love with him. This naturally frustrated Allen and at dinner one evening, he erupted and pointedly said:

"Anne, I think you're afraid of sex."

This time she looked at him. "I suppose you're going to tell me that I'm unawakened . . . that you will change all that."

"Exactly."

She sipped the champagne to avoid his eyes.

"I suppose you've been told this before," he said.

"No, I've heard it in some very bad movies."

"Dialogue is often trite because it's easier to sneer at the truth."

"The truth?"

"That you're afraid of life — and living."

"Is that what you think? Just because I'm not rushing into marriage with you?" There was a hint of a smile in her eyes.

"Do you think it's natural to reach twenty and still be a virgin?"

"Virginity isn't an affliction."

"Not in Lawrenceville, maybe. But then you said you don't want to be like the people in Lawrenceville. So let me give you a few facts. Most girls of twenty aren't virgins. In fact, most of them have gone to bed with guys they weren't even crazy about. Their curiosity and natural sex drive led them to try it. I don't think you've ever even had a decent necking session with a guy. How can you know you don't like something if you haven't tried it? Don't you ever have any urges or feelings about anything? Isn't there anyone you ever unbend with? Have you ever thrown your arms around anyone? Man, woman or child? Anne, I've got to break through to you. I love you. I can't allow you to shrivel away into another New England old maid."[2]

It really doesn't matter that this is only a novel and that Allen Cooper is a fictitious character. It doesn't really matter that the facts belie Allen's assertions about virgins. (*Time* in its September 15, 1967, issue, quoting John H. Gagnon of Indiana University's Institute for Sex Research, points out that 50 percent of all brides are still virgins, and another 25 percent slept only with their prospective mate.)[3] An incredible number of persons *have* read this novel (over five million copies were published in paperback during one month alone). And an immense number of young people *have* heard what Allen says about the unnaturalness of being a virgin at 20. And many of them *have* listened to similar remarks from real people — teachers, classmates, dates. It is hard for them to sift fact from fancy, to know what is right, to decide what is best. They wonder.

The impact of such commonly discussed ideas and the generally sex-permeated atmosphere in the United States does tend to confuse. To further complicate the situation, couples in their teens and 20's are not just that sure of themselves. They are searching for security, striving to attain maturity (as we all are and must continue to do for the rest of our lives), attempting to establish values, to understand one another, to evaluate the relationship which exists between them. Today's world changes daily. They are well aware of that and are trying to find their place in it. To these many factors producing turmoil in young lovers' hearts add the basic physical, emotional attraction present. Sex *is* pleasurable; it is fun, in a sense. Persons in love surely recognize that, but they also feel additionally, at times, an intense compulsion to express physically, sexually, their inner sentiments of tenderness. Everyone knows the easy solution: but is the easy answer the correct one, the one which will best strengthen and deepen their mutual love, the morally right one?

The confused person may be able to dismiss fairly swiftly proposals advocating sex before marriage which his peers offer. True, some tension or awkwardness normally follows from the rejection. "So you are *still* holding the party line, huh?" "Don't you know that is just old school?" "Really, how immature can you be!"

"Would you believe, a virgin!" Darts like that can hurt, cause doubts. But what really disturbs the unsure person in love are the more scientific arguments of writers, lecturers, psychologists.

A college student walks into the campus bookstore, spots a volume called *Unmarried Love,* grabs it eagerly and hopes to find an answer to these very relevant questions zooming around in his mind. "Sexual Wisdom for the Single." So reads the cover. He turns it over in his hands. The black and white photograph of the author, a distinguished-looking scholar, impresses him. He reads the caption: "The Author, Eustace Chesser, widely known psychologist and lecturer, is also the author of *Love Without Fear,* which has sold more than three million copies." Nothing succeeds—or influences — like success. More interested, he glances at the inside flap and catches sentences like ". . . boldly confronts the truth that almost everyone knows, but not everyone admits: a preponderance of young women and men today have love affairs before marriage and sometimes without marrying at all. . . . A new code of sexual behavior is in the making. . . . As no two people are alike, there can be no one rule governing the wisdom or propriety of unmarried love."

Sold.

Back in his room, he devours this easily readable book which delves into areas of great concern for him. The suggestions seem free, reasonable; the arguments, logical enough. He jots down some basic rules:

> "The point I am making is that premarital intercourse in itself is neither moral nor immoral. It can help or retard our growth toward maturity according to our particular makeup. . . .
>
> "There is one indispensable condition: namely, it is always wrong to indulge in premarital intercourse without the use of birth control . . . .
>
> "That is why, for the unmarried, deep petting is often the best method of intimate physical relationship. . . .
>
> "In my opinion the simplest and best help we can give to the unmarried girl with an unwanted pregnancy is to terminate the pregnancy — the

sooner the better, preferably before the resultant bodily and mental changes are fully established and felt."[4]

That is hardly what he was taught at Sunday School or by his parents. And he is not quite certain his girl would buy all of it. And very likely he objects to some of the principles. But he does wonder and he does find it difficult to refute the argumentation.

Later on he reads Harvey Cox's *The Secular City* for a class in sociology. Coming to Chapter 8, "Sex and Secularization," he becomes confused from a different point of view. He could, if he wished to, forget about Chesser on the basis that the psychologist seems to manifest few religious overtones in his book. But Cox is a professor of theology and culture at Andover Newton Theological School. Here a man of God tackles the same general question of premarital sex. However, the answers offered seem vague, even evasive, and surely not pointed like Chesser's. Sentences here and there make him wonder. "I do not believe that an evangelical ethic of premarital sex can be chopped down to a flat answer to this weighted question without impoverishing and distorting it. . . . The reason it cannot be answered once and for all is that circumstances vary from couple to couple. Guidance must be given with specific persons rather than with general conventions in view."[5]

So the sexual climate of our times, the ready views of confreres in school or work, the writings of certain scholars, the inner uncertainty of a young person's mental and emotional life . . . all these combine to create confusion about chastity. Anyone who loves and deals with the young knows the challenge here is acute and no facile, black and white, categorical answers exist. Succeeding paragraphs, then, should be taken as gropings rather than finally conclusive findings.

Guidance from God

A Christian who sees the New Testament coming from the hand of God can discover some divine guidance in this area. The Ten Commandments, of course, speak of adultery and entertaining wrong desires for a neighbor's wife. But such moral precepts do not seem to apply, at least on face value, to the situation we are discussing. The letters of St. Paul to Christians in various cities of the Mediterranean do, however, carry greater relevance. Several of them (1 Cor. 6; Gal. 5; Ephes. 5), contain severe warnings about fornication and fornicators, excluding them from the kingdom of God. Some background and an explanation of one actual text may make this ancient, but still living, message more meaningful.

Jesus was a Jew, as was Paul. They lived in Jewish communities and breathed the Jewish religious and ethical atmosphere. Historians indicate that, in general, Judaism did demand at the time of Christ standards of moral conduct far above anything in the surrounding pagan environment. Prostitution was strictly forbidden and an unmarried girl was supposed to be a virgin. Chastity was held up as the highest of virtues, the crown which should adorn every maiden's head. The man who violated an unsullied woman could be punished severely, either in a financial way or by death itself, depending on the circumstances. In passing, it might be noted that this continued on in marital life. The role of a Jewish married woman in terms of honor and respect stood normally above that of her pagan contemporaries.

Sexual ideals apparently were a little less lofty in the Roman world and especially in Greece. One expert remarks that it would be even fairly safe to say that chastity was nowhere esteemed in the Hellenistic world except among the Jews. Polygamy over many years had diminished esteem for a woman in practice and in law. A man was free to do pretty much what he pleased with impunity. The woman, not so. Unequal partner at home and insignificant outside the house, she stood as second-class citizen even in the upper sections of society. The lack of chastity in a man, married or single, was judged a minor failing, if a fault at all. Homosexuality, incest and other grosser sexual aberrations were not uncommon and often the law or the consensus cast tolerant glances at them. The Roman world's view of woman and chastity rose a bit above the Greek picture but still hardly equaled the elevated Jewish notion.

Christians living in the first century at Corinth understandably found high sexual standards difficult to follow. A commercial city with cosmopolitan status, it was notorious even in ancient times as a hotbed of every kind of vice. "To live like a Corinthian" meant complete moral collapse; "a Corinthian girl" and a "prostitute" were synonymous terms. When St. Paul wrote to the Romans (1:24-32) and sharply catalogued vices, he was at that time in Corinth and could write easily since realistic illustrations abounded around him.

We should hardly be surprised, then, to learn that early followers of Christ, hearing mention of freedom from the law and emphasis on the spirit, misinterpreted these directives. When Paul wrote words like, "All things are lawful, but not all things are expedient," it is little wonder that Corinthian Christians (some of whom were converts from Judaism) accepted this as an approval of the common practices of the city. The idealistic Jewish chastity rules now could be forgotten and the easier, more pleasurable procedures of paganism consecrated to the one, true God. Since legalism was out, then license must be in. Or so they thought and acted until the fiery Apostle dispatched an epistle to them.

> "I write these things not to put you to shame, but to admonish you as my dearest children" (1 Cor. 4:14).
> "It is actually reported that there is immorality among you . . ." (1 Cor. 5:1).
> "Do not err; neither fornicators, nor idolators, nor adulterers, nor the effeminate, nor sodomites, nor thieves, nor the covetous, nor drunkards, nor the evil-tongued, nor the greedy will possess the kingdom of God" (1 Cor. 6:9).[6]

Strong words, indeed. He feels these methods of acting form serious breaches in the Christian way of life, so serious as to exclude those who practice them from membership in the Church and ultimately from the rewards of eternal life with God in the next world.

A man cannot be God's friend and Christ's brother and conduct himself along these lines.

In defending his position and emphasizing the malice of fornication, St. Paul manifests great understanding of sexual relations. In fact, Harvey Cox, whom we have quoted earlier, comments that St. Paul seems to understand sexual intercourse better than Hugh Hefner does.

> "Do you not know that your bodies are members of Christ? Shall I then take the members of Christ and make them members of a harlot? By no means! Or do you not know that he who cleaves to a harlot, becomes one body with her? 'For the two, it says, shall be one flesh.' But he who cleaves to the Lord is one spirit with him" (1 Cor. 6:15-17).[7]

Paul in effect shows that sexual relations between man and woman cannot remain a merely casual affair. A oneness exists so close that it produces a practical identity of flesh. Such a union surely must flow over into the whole being of the persons involved and cannot be limited to a surface entanglement soon to be forgotten. Modern findings of psychology confirm this, particularly in regard to the woman.

Proceeding from this physical, psychological fact of experience, the Apostle rises to a spiritual level and reminds his hearers of their noble dignity. Through faith and baptism they become intimately united with their Lord, Savior, God, Christ Jesus. Bodies elevated to such a sublime degree should never be contaminated with the frequently used body of a prostitute.

It would be hard to question the power and meaning of St. Paul's admonishment to his flock in Corinth. But two people engaged or at least in love, may find this approach of only limited assistance in their current dilemma. The Jewish partner, or the unbelieving one, does not see this biblical excerpt through the eyes of Christian faith. In addition, the conduct reprobated seems to touch prostitution, moral laxity, dissolute living, unnatural vices, practices which cheapen sex, lower it, render it a thing merely to be used. This couple is in love. Sex for them is beautiful and singular, not dirty and universal. They think it is an expression of their own unique love. Not for kicks, nor with any other partner. But reserved for each other alone, and for love. Without rejecting St. Paul and the Bible and God's guidance, let's try a different approach. We may end up at the same destination.

A Married Priest Speaks

When Pope John XXIII summoned the bishops of the world to Rome for the Vatican Council, he "opened the windows" of the Catholic Church to let in some "fresh air." The reforms resulting from Vatican II already have touched almost every American in some way. Not the least of these changes has been an ever-increasing cooperation between Catholic, Protestant, Jewish clergy and laymen. This book, in a modest way, reflects, I trust, that openness of spirit and dialogue. Authors from a wide spectrum of beliefs and backgrounds have been either quoted or consulted.

Fittingly, then, in that tradition, we call upon Robert Farrar Capon, author of *Bed and Board: Plain Talk About Marriage,* to contribute some assistance here. He is eminently qualified to do so. The jacket of his work states that he is "an Episcopal priest, player of music, teacher of Greek, husband, father of six." His instructions to a young couple before marriage offer in pointed, yet pleasant fashion, a few principles to guide them in their courtship.

"A couple of years back there was a cartoon that showed two clams sitting at the bottom of the ocean. One of them says to the other, 'But you wouldn't buy a new car without first driving it, would you?' My premarital couple doesn't crack a smile. Not an eye blinks. Nobody's punch lines fall flatter than a priest's in marriage instructions. As far as they are concerned, I am only supposed to be a 'minister of religion.' Like in the movies. The predictable vicar who thinks life is about afternoon teas and long walks. No matter, I press on. I raise the subject of premarital chastity as such. It is not old-fashioned, I tell them or if it is, it has yet to go out of date as far as the facts are concerned. What do you think you have to practice for marriage? They watch me blankly, but they are watching. Well, you don't have to practice going to bed together. And you don't have to, because you can't. Premarital intercourse is not the same thing as the marriage bed. Of course there is something unique about the first time whenever it comes, but if it comes before, there is inevitably attached to it the fillip of the forbidden. It doesn't matter how enlightened people are, or how blasé the society is; our mores, honored in breach or observance, are our mores, and we're stuck with them. We might as well try to change our air. Do it now, I tell them, and doing it later will have the edge taken off it to say the least. People think of the flesh as a mighty monster straining at the leash, bursting with health and unquenchable vigor. What they don't know is that poor flesh takes an awful drubbing. It's not *all* in the head, but a good bit of it is. Brother Ass is pretty easily confused, and there are a lot of wedding nights that are not nearly as funny as the jokes about them.

"So forget about practicing *that*. I tell them. You'll have plenty of time later. Try to make the start as much of a start as you can. Licit sex usually runs a poor second to illicit; don't make any more comparisons than you can help. What you really need to practice is keeping promises. Right now of course you wouldn't go to bed with anybody else, but later on, it's not always that clear, and then these little exercises in fidelity will be worth something in terms of chastity and trust. So, I say if you have so far been chaste, don't let anyone talk you out of it. And if you haven't been, well, try and cut out the compromises. Even a tardy dose of principle is better than none.

"Well, that usually produces something of a studied silence. I don't try to be embarrassing, but since there is in fact a lot of premarital gun-jumping even among professing Christians, and since it is usually justified with fairly highfalutin reasons, I feel obliged to say it. Fancy reasons or not, it makes an already tricky job even harder. But I also feel obliged to suggest that they do something utterly outlandish besides. I tell them not only to be chaste but to be modest—to cut out not only the intercourse, but all the little semi-moral approximations to it: the petting that everybody takes for granted. Because that doesn't help much either. If it involves any worthwhile and pleasurable discoveries, it would be much more comforting to make them later amid a pile of unpaid bills where they could lighten the load of lifelong monogamy. It is really too bad to fumble one's way through them greedily in the back seat of some car when they could be savored and relished at leisure on a long winter evening. . . ."[8]

It is good to have a man like Capon say this. He is a married man and can speak from personal experience. The critical inquirer may, and often does, summarily dismiss comments on sex from a celibate like myself with a wave of the hand. The dismissal is not usually verbalized, but in substance it says, "How can *you* possibly understand and advise me on sex?" Father Capon cannot be disregarded so easily.

Growth in Love

The preceding lengthy quotation argues for premarital chastity on grounds that do not, at first glance, seem particularly religious. There is no mention of the Bible, no thundering reminder of the Commandment, "Thou shall not commit adultery," no ominous warning about sin. Instead, the couple is told that waiting for sex is the best preparation for a lasting, faithful, fulfilling marriage. This is the kind of advice that modern couples will listen to.

And they do need practical suggestions and sound, deep motivation why they should wait until marriage. The easy approach would be: abandon all control, do what comes naturally, allow inner feelings freely to express themselves in a physical way. To channel, instead, one's sincere affection for a beloved is hard, requires strength and determination.

I have found, as I am sure Father Capon has also, that the best motivating force for the average young man and woman, the motive which can give them sufficient power and courage in this challenge is love. They are now, they feel, deeply in love. They hope to remain in love for the remainder of their days on earth. And they want this wonderful love to grow, even become stronger, not simply diminish and die with the years. To show questioning lovers how a chaste courtship can deepen their mutual love and better prepare them for a lifelong union in marriage gives them valuable resolve when short-lived pleasures pull them in a quite opposite direction.

The following points hardly form an exhaustive list of reasons why and how sexual control before marriage strengthens love. They are, rather, insights which have evolved over the years from contact and conversation with many persons individually, in couples, and in groups.

1. *Risk of self-deception.* The young man and woman who profess their love for one another mean it. Yet the fact stands that many of these furious romances never reach the altar. We really can't help falling in love. But staying in love and seeing that love emerges as the kind that will produce sustained happiness in matrimony is something else.

Most men and women count at least a few broken hearts in the course of their search for a love which would stand the test of married life. This is neither bad, nor unexpected. We learn as we love; we learn from mistakes and failures, and broken hearts, too.

The engaged couple, or the pair who think they are truly in love, question premarital chastity. "We are in love and eventually will marry. Why not?" But can they be sure this love will last? It may. But there is no permanent commitment. Even the ring only symbolizes something in their hearts. And those interior feelings can change and the diamond be returned. It is a heavy risk for them, particularly for the girl who surrenders. In love she gives herself to this fine young man who one day will stand by as husband, father, protector, provider. But later (who can predict when, how or why?) the beautiful love sours, they break up and go their separate ways. What does she tell her next lover?

The understanding priest spends many hours restoring crushed spirits in the young lady absolutely shattered by such an experience. In love, with marriage honestly promised and planned, it seemed perfectly right to yield her heart and body to him. Now that it didn't work out, she recognizes the mistake. As one girl in her 20's put it, "And what about that case in which the engaged couple breaks up? The humiliation would be too much to bear."

What was it that Mephistopheles, with a triumphant sneer, sang in Gounod's *Faust*? "Never give your love so lightly, until you wear his wedding ring."

Couples in love naturally, at moments of tenderness and intimacy, feel this relationship will never break up. But can they be certain? Can the girl, who suffers the brunt of the harmful effects if they do, be sure until there is that permanent, exclusive sealing of their love "until death do us part?" The stakes are high, the risks great.

2. *Danger of retarding love.* In the first three chapters of this book, I attempted to show that love is a giving, a sharing with others. In addition, as this love is directed to a member of the opposite sex, and a particular one at that, it tends to a union with that person. Lovers want to be together. They want to be one. This oneness, however, embraces all levels of their being. True, in sexual intercourse there is a "two in one flesh" union. And, as Dr. Max Levin remarks, "The sex act is the supreme example of an interpersonal relationship."[9] But the union of love goes beyond the surface, the physical. A successful marriage demands, as we have seen, an intellectual, emotional, spiritual, cultural union as well as a physical one. Physical union is normally the easiest to obtain, and ideally should be the last to come. The other unions take time, effort, patience to develop. The physical beautifully expresses them and can deepen and sustain them. But a too quick entrance of the physical union into courtship can retard the birth and growth of those more subtle, but more

stable and permanent unions.

Marriage manuals stress constantly the need for deepening a surface love between two people. A spontaneous, warm glow may spark the romance. This beginning affection may grow, more or less quickly depending on the people involved and the characteristics of their dating patterns. However, that hot, physical love does not always indicate a happy married love. There is so much more to marriage than sexual intercourse. Wedded life is not simply going to bed together, but living together all day, every day, the rest of your life. There are 24 hours in a day, possibly eight of which are spent in bed. And how many of those are dedicated to mutual sexual lovemaking?

The movies have not always helped. Their often dreamy vision of love, immediate on first sight and ending happily ever after, pushes most adolescents into a world of fantasy. The harsh realities of interpersonal relationships, the adjustments necessary in marriage, the sufferings and crises which actually prove a couple's love, seldom come into the picture. The girl expects to be swept off her feet; the boy anticipates beautiful young things wilting before him. Their notions of married life follow similar patterns.

The main thrust of marriage courses and premarriage classes probably should tackle this false notion. Young men and women need to see sex in its proper focus — a factor magnificent, beautiful, warm, tender, unifying, supportive — but not all of married life by a long shot. It is an expression of love, not love itself. Senior citizens after 50 years of matrimony may seldom, if ever, engage in sexual relations. But no one questions the real love existing between them.

The time for courting and for engagement should be spent deepening a couple's mutual understanding of each other. They need to know each other, and well. They also need to meet relatives on both sides, to discuss an almost limitless number of issues — religion, politics, work, education, children, finances, furniture, music, likes, dislikes, to learn one another's moods, to appreciate mutual hopes and aspirations, fears and failures. In short they need to know each other as persons, rich individuals, many-faceted personalities. This task never ends. We humans are just so complex that we are always striving to understand others. But the better we know a partner, the more we can love him. And the more this knowledge and love comes before the nuptials, the better the prospects for marriage.

To foster this, we encourage couples to date in calm, unexciting situations. Dances, movies, dinner, athletic events — these all have their place. But a courtship exclusively limited to these never permits them really to know each other. A third element — the game, the dance, etc. — always exists to sustain their interests. Quiet evenings at each other's homes enable them to see the partner in his or her relaxed, normal environment and appreciate how the loved one relates to brothers, sisters, parents.

A love affair which runs away physically suffers the same dangers. One disillusioned lass commented, "Love him, don't make love to him. It spoils everything. I know. And I regret it so much. We got caught up with each other's bodies and forgot about the minds, the ambitions, the wonders." The intoxicating ecstasy of sexual relations, and the heavy petting which approximates it, makes it difficult for a couple to explore calmly the mysterious depths of each other's personalities. Once tasted, the urge to repeat grows insistently. A restlessness to be home, to be alone, to be one with each other can spoil or at least diminish the full enjoyment of other activities.

Then, too, one or both of the partners may begin to wonder just how deep is their relationship when the physical has been frequently and strongly a part of the courtship. Every marriage is a risk; no one can be sure of matrimonial bliss. Someone asked King Arthur in *Camelot* if he doubted the success of the Round Table. The noble, idealistic king responded, "Only fools never doubt." So, also, only foolish, shallow men would wait at the altar without some hesitation, some doubt about the future; only foolish, overly optimistic women would march down the aisle without some questions, some anxiety. These doubts are intensified when there has been little control of physical desires in courtship. The man may ask himself, "Do I really love her? Or is it her body I want and love?" And the woman may say to herself, "Does he really love me? Does he want me for what I am? Or is it my body that he seeks?" They really cannot be sure until much later. And, again, the risks are enormous.

Needless to say, the couple who experience intense guilt feelings after such activities find the learning process in courtship even more complicated. They tend to overstress sex itself, wrestle with the remorse which plagues them, and yearn for marriage which will "make it legal." It is then for psychiatrists and psychologists to explore the harm done to their emotional life and to discover the various ways in which these scars show in later life.

A romance like this is exciting, tingling, yes; mature, deep, auguring well for life together in marriage, we wonder. Too much of anything spoils it. Sex cannot be excepted. The couple who become overinvolved may grow tired of sex, tend to identify it with love instead of viewing it as a good, unique expression of love, and ultimately ruin both their love and their appreciation of sex's proper role in human life.

3. *Respect for the one loved.* Love and respect, as we saw earlier in the book, go together. At least it seems impossible for a person to love someone without respecting him. The close interaction which arises when couples fall in love demands respect for the feelings and principles of one another. Otherwise, the whole relationship collapses. Marriage, and courtship leading to that state, is not a one-way street. Communication probably heads the list as the most important element in every marital union. Without honest dialogue between two people, sincere friendships cannot blossom. Eventually, hurt feelings, misunderstandings, bitterness, even hate arise when two people do not openly discuss their conflicts and respect each other's opinions.

Such general rules for personal relationships bear special application to the question we are discussing. The boy, for example, may judge his sweetheart's views on sex before marriage outdated or rigid. He may really believe that sexual intercourse before the wedding day could foster their mutual love, cement their relationship, and better prepare them for life together. She disagrees. And strongly. . .

Why she holds the opinions she does is complicated indeed. Religious training from early days, parental guidance, the customs of our culture, a woman's intuitive hesitation — who can spot the cause, or even isolate it? But the fact remains that she wants to wait. Violating principles she has established would certainly cause pain, very likely tears, and normally extreme guilt feelings. It is too late for her to change. He should recognize and accept that.

Exerting pressure to capitulate when she clearly feels such behavior offends her conscience hardly manifests deep respect. The girl may rightly question the sincerity of his love since regard for her views and her dignity as an individual does not seem to exist here. And later on in marriage? Will he roughly dismiss her dissenting opinions on other matters like finances, training of the children, church attendance, recreation?

Esteem for her views on premarital sex proves his love; constant bickering about them at least raises doubts about the depth of it. Even Dr. Chesser, quoted earlier, whose guidelines in courtship are surely not the ones maintained in this book, agrees with us. He insists that honesty and respect for the feelings of the other partner are probably the fundamental commandment in his modern code of ethics.

4. *Unsatisfactory premarital sexual experience may permanently affect a couple's appreciation of similar actions in marriage.* Sexual intercourse before marriage is not the same as afterward. There are a multiplicity of factors which can, from a purely physical, emotional, aesthetical aspect, render this action less pleasant, or even painful and troublesome. Such traumatic surroundings may affect the attitude of the married pair later on with respect to sexual relations.

Dr. Evelyn Millis Duvall's book, *Why Wait Till Marriage?* succinctly describes elements which can make premarital sex highly unfulfilling. I quote at random but at length because of the excellence of her treatment.

"First sex experiences are often disappointing. The fellow becomes too excited too quickly. He may appear impotent or unable to sustain an erection long enough at first. It takes time for a girl to awaken sexually before she too can respond. She must become gradually accustomed to sexual activity before she finds it even comfortable . . .

"Boys tend to be body-centered, and girls are person-centered from the first. Thus, their premarital experiences can be frustrating. The boy may go through with it, but without the satisfaction her response would have brought him. The girl may attempt to match his enthusiasm, but be left unsatisfied, unawakened, or uneasy. . .

"Because each feels a little anxious and a little guilty, the girl is likely to be frigid and the boy at least partially impotent. They may be left with the feeling that they are inadequate human beings when the very thing they set out to prove was their competence.

"Fear of discovery keeps many an unmarried couple from full enjoyment of their intimacy. Because it is generally considered wrong, the boy and girl approach each other with anxiety. Their ears are alert for any possible witness to their indiscretion. Their attention cannot be entirely upon each other, so long as they are afraid of being caught. Even if what they are doing has gone undetected so far, there is always the danger that somehow someone will find out. . .

"The need for concealment of premarital sexual intercourse gives little or no security to the relationship. . .

"Haste is a risk for many an unmarried couple. Pleasure in sexual intimacy requires a sense of leisure all too often lacking before marriage. A man and wife can look forward to long, quiet evenings together. They can take the time for the mutual loving and being loved that bring fulfillment to them both. They can prepare for their coming together with all the pleasant accompaniments that make their relationship throb with significance. Soft music, their favorite scents, special arrangements that heighten their pleasure in each other can be arranged in advance. Their lovemaking is in their own bed, amidst surroundings that they have lovingly prepared. A married couple's sex life can be richly varied and full of ritual because they have time to develop a repertoire of response to one another. . .

The young pair before marriage all too often have to snatch what they can get where they can get it. Their contact is suffused with urgency. The girl, and often the boy too, is left unsatisfied even after having gone through the motions of going all the way. . . ."[10]

This powerful testimony from Dr. Duvall is sometimes countered by the argument that sexual compatibility of a man and a woman for each other cannot be established without some premarital experiences. Despite her strong description of the risks and liabilities, such reasoning may seem plausible enough. But one asks if premarital sexual relations are really necessary or even effective in establishing sexual compatibility. A proper medical examination before marriage, thought by many doctors to be highly commendable, might reveal physical obstacles. Psychological impediments do exist, but is sex before marriage a means of determining and curing them? An affirmative answer is hardly the universal judgment of today's medical profession. The problems involved are far too hidden and complex to admit of such a facile solution.

5. *Risk of selfishness.* Love and selfishness are mutually exclusive. The couple in love want their love to grow. Anything which fosters selfishness tends to weaken that love which they have for each other. There is a double risk of feeding selfishness in courtship through premarital sexual experiences.

First of all, it is possible, particularly in teen-age dating situations and the early stages of courtship, for a man and a woman to use each other. The overly aggressive boy who fails to contain emotional, physical urges can be using his girl, catering to his baser instincts and, in fact, acting very selfishly. Similarly, but more subtly, the young woman who permits her friend to run out of control, or even leads him to that point, can be surrendering to a selfish desire for attention and affection. She, in effect, may be using her boyfriend.

The danger of such selfishness creeping into a relationship always lurks near. Only the two involved can decide if it is a real love that motivates their physical embrace, or a mere desire for some pleasure. And sometimes they cannot determine that until much later in life. But they must constantly ask the question. This is not to imply that every time two lovers make love, physically, outside of marriage they are being selfish toward each other. A distinguished Catholic psychologist, now teaching in an Eastern seminary, once, in reply to a pointed question, commented that premarital sexual intercourse could be an act of love in the strict, psychological sense of the word. Sincere self-giving could be present. Quite obviously the possibility of this is much stronger in couples who are mature in age and attitude and whose courtship has extended over a relatively long period of time.

Secondly, looking at this same action from its possible life-creating effect, we might say that the two lovers, though not selfish toward each other, may be acting selfishly toward the child that could result from their lovemaking. Contemporary studies indicate the importance of love, security, warmth in early childhood years, even in prenatal days, for the eventual full maturity, growth and happiness of a person. The child conceived through a premarital union certainly cannot enjoy the totally secure atmosphere desired. Regardless of the particular circumstances and despite a better understanding today on the part of parents and those affected, tensions still do exist when a woman is pregnant and unmarried. Even if the couple rejoices over the conception, advances the date of the marriage, showers the child with all possible love and affection, there still remain certain difficulties and anxieties. There may be a shaky financial situation, an awkwardness in dealing with others, a hesitation about informing and hurting disappointed parents, a frantic rush to obtain the license, find an apartment and complete arrangements with some clergyman, a worry about disturbed educational plans.

Are couples in this instance offering their first child

the environment he or she should have? Can we not say, then, that they have neglected their responsibilities as future parents? Is this selfishness, not toward each other, but toward the child? Are they selfish parents?

Naturally, the rapid development and spread of contraceptive devices may, for some couples, seem to eliminate the danger of a selfish, premarital conception. The Syracuse University *Daily Orange,* in an editorial on "The Pill" remarked, "The pill has eliminated the fear of pregnancy. No longer can a coed use pregnancy as any reason for refusing to have intercourse."[11] One wonders if the editor, in his understandable enthusiasm for the "pill," has not oversimplified the case.

For example, a study of illegitimate births from 1940 through 1965 by Arthur A. Campbell of the U.S. Public Health service and James D. Cowhig of the Welfare administration reveals some interesting facts. In 1940 there were 89,500 illegitimate births; in 1965, the total amounted to 291,200. This might not seem significant in view of our population growth, but even the overall illegitimacy rate has increased.[12]

We can also inquire if lovers before marriage carefully and with premeditation always equip themselves before each date. Some rather objective testimony indicates that many women prefer to be swept off their feet and carried romantically into this act rather than to prepare in a calculated and protected manner for the evening's lovemaking.

Of course, couples who find the use of contraceptives either a violation of their conscience and moral principles or feel they in some way diminish the total self-giving desired in sexual intercourse must consider even more seriously the question of possible parenthood and the selfish overtones of it in their unmarried state.

To give the *Daily Orange* editor his proper credit, the danger of pregnancy is less today and less a motivation for premarital chastity. It should be evident from my presentation in this chapter that I do not judge it to be one of the more cogent reasons for sexual control before marriage. Nevertheless, as the facts testify, the possibility does continue to exist and must be dealt with. Strangely enough, I have found in giving a number of lectures on college campuses that mention of the pregnancy possibility brings attentive looks from the audience. Apparently, despite our sophistication and mechanical (or chemical) advances, many young adults still do wait until they marry because of fear of pregnancy.

6. *Strengthening the nuptial vows.* Father Capon remarked earlier that what a couple really needs to practice before marriage is not sexual intercourse, but keeping promises. His comment is well taken. The essence of marriage is this—to promise, to make a solemn vow, to offer one's heart and soul and body to the beloved for life. There is a commitment made here, before God and other men, to live and give in sickness and in health, for richer or for poorer, for better or for worse.

Notice that the promise is made before God and men. It can be made secretly, privately, between the two lovers. But to quote the *Dutch Catechism,* "As long as the bond has not been confirmed by Church and State, it is not definitive."[13] The ceremony of marriage, then, is not some external action which simply "makes it legal." It is, instead, the unveiling to others of an inner promise. It tells the world that this man and woman now publicly before their Maker and their fellowmen vow to share each other's lives together. They embrace a common future with all of its hopes and disappointments, its pleasures and its pains, its joys and sorrows, its successes and its failures. Only death will cut the cord which now joins them.

The husband and wife who so seal hearts and hopes together at the altar, join their bodies together in the marriage bed. Sexual intercourse makes their lifelong promise more definitive, it deepens their commitment to each other, it physically expresses their total union.

Keeping the promises will not always be easy. Nor will the days and years ahead be ever joyful. Pain, weariness, boredom, restlessness, irritation, being taken for granted — these and how many other enemies will seek to weaken and destroy the nuptial vows.

The man and woman who have saved the joys and delights of sexual intercourse until after they have made this public promise should find the deepening of it somewhat easier. They have not experienced the total pleasure of sexual intercourse until marriage. For them, this action reinforces the nuptial commitment. It tends to be associated only with this man, my husband, or this woman, my wife. And it is seen only in a context of home, family, security, joint living together. Anticipated before marriage, these intimacies, beautiful and thrilling as they are, lose some of their uniqueness. This is probably what the unlettered girl means when she fears that "It won't be special" after they are married if they sleep together before.

All of this has additional meaning for the religious person. For the believing Jew, marriage speaks to him of the love between Yahweh and Israel. The love in marriage is a giving-receiving relationship; the love of Yahweh for His People is the same. He loves and protects them, He will be their God, if they respond with love, service and faithfulness. They then become His People and there exists a sacred covenant between them and Yahweh. The marriage covenant thus both speaks to men of a hidden, deeper reality — the relationship between God and men — and at the same time is given an added sacred value through its comparison with that holy relationship between Yahweh and His People.[14]

For the believing Christian, a further religious meaning is added to the nuptial vows. He sees marriage as a sign of God's love and union with man and this world in Jesus Christ. The coming of God's Son to earth, His assuming human flesh is viewed as a wedding of God and man. Again, God loves and gives His Son — and man believes and accepts this gift. In return, man is to give back faith, love, trust and is to demonstrate that responsive love through service of others.

In addition, for those Christians who consider marriage a grace-giving sacrament, the nuptial promise contains within it the power to communicate the Holy Spirit to husband and wife. Since the sacred sign of this sacrament is the mutual promise and the life lived in accordance with that promise, it follows that all the love, tenderness, help and counsel which partners in marriage offer each other become for them sources of grace, of Christ's presence, of the Holy Spirit.[15]

Jesuit poet-priest Daniel Berrigan writes eloquently about these sign-sacrament aspects of marriage in *They Call Us Dead Men*.[16]

If sexual intercourse, reserved until marriage, has value in strengthening the nuptial promises for any person, religious or not, then even more does premarital chastity have a purpose for Jewish and Christian couples who view matrimony as a uniquely sacred bond and a mysteriously profound sign of God's relationship with men.

* * * *

Dr. Max Levin, in a lecture on "The Meaning of Sex and Marriage: A Lecture to College Students" appearing in the *Current Medical Digest,* has this to say about sex before marriage: "The physician is not a religious teacher and he does not speak on grounds of morality. He speaks from the standpoint of health, which includes emotional health. From this standpoint I submit that the desirable ideal is premarital chastity."[17]

Why wait until marriage? I join with Dr. Levin and Episcopalian Father Robert Capon and scholar-writer Dr. Evelyn Duvall in replying — because premarital chastity can be most helpful in keeping one's inner peace, in deepening a couple's mutual love, and in preparing for a successful and happy marriage.

6. How Far Can We Go?

*A*nn Phillips may have been wrestling with a person in the car's front seat along the shore of Lake Delta on that summer evening. But more, she was grappling with a problem. "Don't you really love me?"

The question confused her. He loves her, she does love him. Then why wait? Why not go all the way, now, before marriage? The previous chapter tried to offer some help in solving that puzzle. But let's presume Tony and Ann accepted all the reasons I gave. Let's presume also they have established a definite goal for themselves — no sexual intercourse until after the nuptial vows. A second question still remains unanswered in her mind. How far can we go? Or is it, how far should we go? How far, that is, without hurting our relationship with each other and with God? The present chapter will treat those questions.

The discussion will become somewhat involved. I want to sketch here, therefore, the overall plan I intend to follow. First of all, it seems to me quite essential to establish the fundamental need and consequent value of self-control in every person's life. And sexual control is a part of that general self-mastery. Next I hope to show the delicate nature of my task — to steer the middle course between a view on the one hand that offers excessively rigid rules of courtship and an opinion on the other that gives a practically ruleless "free-love" code of sexual morality. Finally, in the theoretical discussion of our topic, I want briefly to touch on the philosophy of situational ethics as it applies in this matter.

The ensuing more practical and concrete discussion will offer a few background principles, then a sort of master code for guidance, and, last, suggested guidelines to cover specific matters such as necking and petting.

Self-control

In an earlier chapter I summarily described growth that goes on during the teen-age years. The goal sought is maturity, a goal that means self-understanding, self-acceptance, self-identity, self-control. Sexual control is a part of it. And all of these elements are quite interrelated. What fosters growth in one area promotes it in the other. Cardinal Suenens in his book, *Love and Control,* succinctly remarks, "Whatever can help a person gain self-control in general can help him gain sexual mastery of himself."[1] Later on in the same work he describes how man has used his mind and body to bring the universe under control. We have explored, examined and harnessed the forces and elements in this world to serve our needs. Growth, in an individual, a nation, a race, thus demands control.

Dr. Duvall, whom I have cited earlier, clearly describes what is at issue in this question of self and sexual control:

"No one can let his feelings run wild, doing just what he pleases all the time. As you mature, you have to learn how to control yourself in order to live with others. When you were young, your parents controlled your behavior. Now it is up to you to manage yourself. This is true of all aspects of your life. Your self-control is an important part of your personality — in managing your time, budgeting your money, getting along with your friends, and governing your sex behavior.

"There is no evidence that self-control hurts your sex life. Quite the contrary tends to be true. . . .

"This is so in many areas of life. Electricity, for instance, is a great natural force. But, running wild as lightning, it can burn down a building in a great blazing holocaust. It can ruin in a few minutes what has taken years to build and develop. It can, and often does, destroy that which is most precious to man and nature. Yet lightning is 'natural,' uncontrolled, electric power. That same energy through the wires of your home can provide light and heat for years. Electricity under control can cook your food, warm your home in winter and cool it in summer, bring in the magic of radio and television, and keep the wheels of industry whirring through the years.

"Sex, like electricity, can run wild and out of control. Or properly channeled it, too, can light and heat your life through the years. It can destroy others, hurt your loved ones, and damage your children, or it can bless all who have anything to do with you."[2]

I suppose there still are some who would disagree with this, scholars who feel that any control of sex is injurious to the person. But their number seems to be declining. My readings indicate that today more and more educators, physicians, psychiatrists recognize the value and healthiness of sex control. They term a person mature for whom sex does not "run wild and out of control" but rather is "properly channeled."

The young woman (and man) pondering the issue of "How far can we go?" faces a hard, cold fact — control. And control means discipline, limits, boundaries beyond which we do not go, desires that, for the present, we forsake. This brings with it some pain and self-denial and demands imaginative planning. But don't most worthwhile goals in life require all of these?

Two Extremes

Writing this particular chapter is a delicate, difficult and dangerous task. If I offer some fairly rigid and practical rules, the proponent who stresses "love" as the all-determining factor will cry "legalism." If I fail to offer specific guidelines, the men and women involved, particularly the younger ones, will put the book down unsatisfied, complaining that still another adult has ducked the real issues and hidden behind vague generalities. Still again, if I fail to give some "absolute" rules and laws, the conservative moralist will shout "situational ethics" or "relativism" or whatever. A good friend of mine, a moral theologian of note, wrote, when I began this book, "I don't think I would have the courage to tackle this subject." He meant, of course, that the topic is highly controversial and any position will invite criticism. It would be noble to think that courage pushes me on; I hope it is not foolishness.

Fools *do* rush in where angels fear to tread. But my daily experience with young Americans has me deeply convinced that they are looking for answers. They want suggestions, guidelines that are definite and concrete but which also respect their unique individuality and personal freedom. I hope, of course, that mine may do just that.

It is a middle course I wish to follow. I want to avoid an extreme legalism, a collection of rigoristic courtship codes that tie the young and old up in emotional knots and doubts and burden them with unnecessary guilt feelings.

James Kavanaugh is, now, a well-known angry and acidly critical priest-writer. His book, *A Modern Priest Looks at His Outdated Church,* appeared first in digest form as an article in *Look* and soon became a national best seller. A chapter of this volume, "The Rules of Courtship," attacks the legalistic rules, the unduly mechanical and artificial laws on dating so often associated with priests, sisters, and the Catholic Church in general. I want to avoid them. I think I have in my personal presentation of them in class, in lectures, in confession, in personal counseling.

I do not wish to impose a code of conduct which creates such an attitude in a girl that "she would like to spring loose from a system of morality which measures hugs and times kisses, but her fear of hell's fire sends her back into line." I do not want a young woman to become so preoccupied with the question of ". . . to French kiss or not to French kiss" that "keeping the teeth closed becomes the ancient badge of the martyrs who refused to sacrifice to the pagan gods of Rome," and leaves her so anxious that "she firms her lips and guards her tongue with all the ardor of a convent under siege." I do not intend to offer mechanical rules which state that "passionate kissing is marked by the gradual replacing of a love purr with a bearish growl" or that a kiss lasting "twenty seconds might be prolonged." I do not approve of a casuistical attitude in the young who ". . . want to know the borderline of mortal and venial sin . . ." who "probe to discover how far they can go — to drain every ounce of pleasure and experience without offending God." I do not offer to categorize "the first kiss of the sweaty-fingered sopho-more," or to compel young lovers to "submit their romance to a slide rule" or to "measure their kisses and touches with . . . impersonal theorems. . . " Instead, I hope my directions might "be those of one who is guiding a personal conscience, and not the decisions of one who has absorbed it."[3]

In total opposition to this excessive legalism is unfettered freedom to do whatever you want — no restrictions, no limitations, none, that is, other than, possibly, mutual agreement between the two partners. We talked about that casual approach in earlier pages, and rejected it. But coming back nearer the center is the approach increasingly common among religious authors. Petting is neither condemned nor condoned. It depends on the persons involved. Premarital sexual intercourse is neither approved nor discouraged. Its value and moral appropriateness can be judged only in terms of the couple. Does it help their total relation-ship? Do they grow as individuals, as a couple through their intimacy? Is there a deep love relationship al-ready present that seeks and finds best expression in deep petting or sexual relations? Or would this foster in the particular couple selfishness and diminish their love? Harvey Cox, cited in the preceding chapter, seems to approach the question in this manner. So does Richard F. Hettlinger.

Mr. Hettlinger served for four years as a Protestant chaplain at Kenyon, a liberal arts college for men. During the course of that chaplaincy he naturally faced the student's dilemma of sex with all of its ramifica-tions. Apparently like myself, he sought to offer his students some realistic answers to these pressing con-cerns and, later, to put them down in written form. I noticed an advertisement for *Living With Sex: The Student's Dilemma* several months ago, at a time when I was midway through my own efforts with this man-uscript. I quickly purchased his book, anxious to com-pare notes. As could be expected, we cover a good bit of similar ground. But there are differences. His book is addressed to men, mine is directed to both men and women; he rarely illustrates principles or truths with concrete examples, mine, very likely to the distraction, even irritation of the older reader, frequently seeks to exemplify them with practical illustrations. I liked his book very much, found it helpful, readable, informative, and am using it explicitly and otherwise in many instances through this chapter. At the same time, I disagree with some of his conclusions and his approaches in guiding individuals or couples. The differences are real, but still we are not tremendously far apart. This will be evident in a moment.

As I indicated, Hettlinger mirrors an increasingly common approach by Christian moralists to the question of premarital chastity. On prenuptial intercourse, he has this to say:

> "What I have tried to do is to show what the score is, if the expression can be pardoned. I have argued, in brief, that there is no evidence to show that premarital intercourse is either necessary for a successful marriage or more probable to lead to it, that there are some considerations to show that intercourse is best engaged in within the marriage commitment, but that in certain circumstances exceptions may be justifiable or even beneficial. Whether any individual can or should claim such circumstances, and whether in his case it will prove to be a valid claim, I do not know — and indeed he will not either until long after."[4]

On premarital lovemaking short of sexual intercourse, he comments:

> "At what point in the relationship of two people who are not yet married such intimacies as petting to climax or oral-genital contact are appropriate or justifiable, only the mature and responsible couple themselves can decide."[5]

This is hardly the extreme of total "free love," nor does it succumb to the rigors of mechanical courtship rules. It is somewhere in the middle. As I understand Mr. Hettlinger, he argues that it is better, generally, for couples to avoid premarital intercourse and deep, heavy petting. But he would not hesitate, after presenting several cautionary remarks, to advise mature, responsible couples who judge this kind of activity appropriate for themselves to proceed without concern. I am not personally ready to counsel in that way. To argue, after the fact, that human weakness, personal love or cultural pressures diminished or absolved a couple from responsibility on a given occasion, it seems to me, is one thing. To suggest, beforehand, that premarital intercourse or deep petting for them is permissible is another. I would be swift to reassure a troubled couple about their "indiscretion" and quick to minimize the gravity of their lack of control. On the other hand, I would be hesitant to suggest that they stop trying, that they forget about discipline, that they simply give in to the petting.

Mr. Hettlinger mentions that it is exceptionally difficult to be objective about our own sexual life. "There is no field of human activity in which it is so easy to deceive oneself and be convinced by arguments which are in fact nothing but rationalizations of clamant desires."[6] In addition, as can be noted in the lengthy quotation, he holds it is extremely difficult, even impossible, here and now for the individual or couple to know if the circumstances and conditions are such as to warrant an exception for them permitting premarital sex. Some time ago *Time* typically expressed this difficulty, with words to the effect that it is awfully hard to judge if this is true love when the couple is passionately involved in the back seat of a car on a warm summer evening.

Because these risks are real and the possible effects seriously harmful, I would then, in practice, not go as far as Hettlinger does in his advice to the mature couple in love. I will describe what I would tell them, practically speaking, after I discuss the matter of situaation ethics as it applies to premarital chastity.

Situation Ethics

The phrase "situation ethics" strikes fear in the hearts of many Roman Catholic priests. Back in 1952 Pope Pius XII spoke out against situational ethics several times, and a few years later the Holy Office issued some similar warnings. Because these admonitions were general and directed to a mentality rather than to specific individuals and writings, the reaction to them became confused and highly emotional. The very mention of the words placed and, to an extent, still continues to place a man under suspicion.

The fact of the matter is, however, that Roman Catholic moralists have always upheld a certain situational ethic. Laws may be absolute guidelines. But the primacy of conscience as the ultimate norm of "rightness or wrongness" has never been denied. Also, the culpability of an individual with regard to the violation of commandments and precepts has always been measured in terms of awareness and freedom. This is to say that unless the person knows what he is doing is wrong and freely selects to do it he cannot be accused of sin. Finally, the further one wanders from general commandments and fundamental moral principles, the more the individual conscience must determine exactly what is the right and the wrong thing to do in a particular instance. Only he knows and can evaluate all of the circumstances and factors which surround a given situation. These are statements that Roman Catholic priests normally understand and accept.

Father Louis Monden, S.J., in his *Sin, Liberty and Law* explains what I have just said in these words:

> "Within these limits — and although the term has acquired a bad reputation because of the abuses to which it has led — we must clearly affirm with the great classical authors that Catholic morality is, in fact, a *situation ethics*. Once a man has sufficiently formed his conscience by attending to the law of nature and grace, by purifying his intention and gathering solid information, there comes a moment when God's personal invitation on the concrete situation is something no mere legality can wholly discern."[7]

The reason we cannot solve the moral questions of the world with nice, neat formulas is the enormous complexity of man and his universe. Father Charles E. Curran well describes in *Christian Morality Today* the uniqueness of a person and the complex judgments he must make.

> "God has called each person by his own name. In one sense, every individual is unique; every concrete situation is unique. The Christian's answer to the divine call must correspond to his individual circumstances. . .
>
> "Reality is complex. The problems of conscience are complex. Frequently, there are no easy solutions. After prayerful consideration of all values involved, the Christian chooses what he believes to be the demands of love in the present situation. The Christian can never expect to have perfect, mathematical certitude about his actions. The virtue of humility preserves him from falling into the opposed extremes of introspective anxiety and mere formalism. . . ."[8]

I like to believe that the guidelines for courtship which follow correspond to what both Father Monden and Father Curran would call a correct Catholic situation ethics. I hope they preserve the unique, individual responsibility to judge in the ultimate, particular, concrete situation. At the same time, I hope they offer some definite guiding norms which may help an individual and a couple avoid self-deception and unnecessary anxiety.

Background Principles

There are several fundamental truths which the man or woman attempting to judge how far he, or she, or they can go should understand as background material for making this decision.

1. *Honest care and affection should always be present.* This flows quite naturally from our discussion in an earlier chapter on the philosophy of casual sex or sex for kicks. It has been my contention throughout that sex is sacred and sublime, something special. Using sex just for the fun of it does not fit into this picture at all. A priest-psychologist, writing in a weekly journal, summed it up with the remark that sex without love is the real sin. My experience with both

high school and college students confirms that more and more of these young men and women feel exactly this way. What can truly depress a girl is a rather promiscuous sexual affair. She might justify going far or all the way with a boy she loves or at least thinks she loves; she regrets bitterly giving in to a quite casual situation that went out of control. Hettlinger, I think, makes the point strongly in his statement, "Necking above the waist purely for private pleasure or lust can hardly be defended on any grounds."

2. *Sex is serious.* This too flows logically from what I said before. If the powers to love and to create new life are among man's noblest possessions, then tampering with them or using them irresponsibly is a serious matter. José de Vinck in his book, *The Virtue of Sex,* presents a positive approach to sexuality. He details the beauty of sex and in no way embraces the antisex, antipleasure, antibody philosophy of so many ancient writers. Still, he recommends that we should take our sinning a little more seriously. The sin of sex, De Vinck remarks, often stems from a lack of fortitude rather than from ill will or premeditation. Nevertheless, because sex touches the human person deeply and fundamentally and is ordained for a very lofty end, failures in this area produce a guilt which is proportionately severe.[9]

These remarks, seemingly heavy-handed and overly censorious, should receive some clarification and added justification in the next principle.

3. *The girl can be hurt.* When we read or hear a statement like this our thoughts immediately turn to unwed mothers or to some poor young woman with an unwanted pregnancy. The potential hurt and harm for both mother and child is in such instances real and ever present. Each time I spend an hour or two at the office attempting to bring rays of hope into the heart of a depressed, pregnant, unmarried girl, each time I quietly and quickly witness the marriage vows of a nervous groom and his expectant bride, each time I try to console a sobbing feminine voice in the confessional, each time I observe crushed parents bravely holding back tears as with heavy heart they stand in support of their daughter hurriedly entering into a lifetime of

marriage — each time these things happen, I am inwardly irked at the scholars, or the theoreticians, or even the inexperienced but sophisticated advocates of "free love" who talk so glibly about sex.

An unwanted pregnancy is the obvious hurt to the girl. But the harm to her emotional health, while more subtle, can be equally devastating. Dr. Max Levin remarked in a recent lecture, "It is the girl who has so much to lose." The boy and girl after a terminated love affair in which there was some deep physical involvement, may both carry broken hearts. But the girl suffers a compound fracture, Dr. Levin feels, while the boy suffers only a simple one. Dr. Mary Calderone, director of the Sex Information and Educational Council of the United States, in a quote from Mr. Hettlinger's book, cautions the young male about the profound effect sexual relations can have upon his companion:

> "Before you make love to a girl, you have an obligation to come to a deliberate decision in full awareness that you will be setting in motion powerful forces in that girl. If you are concerned about her as a human being, you must decide whether or not it is appropriate at her age and stage of development to learn sexual response. And you must decide whether she is ready for this. If you think she is, then you should acknowledge that it will certainly affect her life to some degree, and perhaps more profoundly than you can imagine."[10]

The issue of emotional harm to a girl stemming from premarital sexual activity is a complex one. One can ask if such harm does occur, and how, and how much. I am neither answering these questions nor suggesting pat solutions to them. My only point is to maintain that the girl can be hurt in different ways and the boy must be aware of this and of his responsibility to her. The answer to the question, "How far can you go?" is not "As far as you can get."

4. *The girl tends to be more mature and under control.* Chapter two, which discussed the differences be-

tween a man and a woman, touched on this point. It carries, however, particular significance when applied to the concrete situation I am discussing in the present section. Mr. Hettlinger notes, "Because her total physical and psychic being reaches maturity earlier than the boy's, the girl is often the more sophisticated socially and the better able to direct a relationship in the initial stages."[11] This is frequently verified in early dating patterns. The girl seems calm, cool and collected, keeping her boyfriend under control. That fact can lead us erroneously to place the responsibility of chastity upon female shoulders. Girls resent this and judge it to be an unfair burden. Constantly fighting off an aggressive young warrior is hardly a delightful pastime, although some may enjoy the challenge and even the game of it. Nevertheless the girl, as a general rule, does seem to have less difficulty in maintaining some direction over her emotions.

After a deep love relationship develops, this is not always the case. Given the right combination of circumstances, she may suddenly be quite willing to let herself go. Mr. Hettlinger describes the boy's confusion who, "having depended largely upon her greater maturity and restraint to maintain the limits of intimacy, . . . may be thrown off kilter by the sudden change in power and give way to impulses which he will regret more than she."[12]

While keeping in mind this exception, I think we can still safely say that the girl usually tends to be under better control. The fact that the boy generally becomes aroused more swiftly and easily than the girl affects the judgment she should make about how intimate they can or should be. It is also the reason for the particular phrasing of the overall norm I will give in a moment.

5. *Younger persons need more detailed guidelines.* Father Kavanaugh, despite his sharp criticisms of traditional Roman Catholic training for courtship, does recognize this. He writes, "Perhaps the adolescent will need more pointed directions, but even he will know new freedom to make mistakes, and will not fear the independence of moral judgment that must attend age and experience."[13] In an earlier paragraph he also re-

marks that "the young do not wish to ignore our directions for dating and courtship. They would even welcome them."[14]

Self-deception is the basic reason we all need specific guidelines in moral matters and why adolescents especially require them. It is never easy to know if we love God and our neighbor or if, instead, we actually are serving and falsely loving ourselves. Father Curran treats the question of laws:

> "Why then is it necessary to have detailed, particular external expressions of these laws? Why a code? Man's love of God is not yet perfect. Fallen human nature still experiences the tendency to self and not to God. . . . Man in his present state cannot know perfectly what the demands of love of God are. Particular, external expressions of the law of love and natural law have a value only insofar as they point out the minimum and basic demands of the law of love."[15]

If these things can be said of the mature adult, how much more can we affirm them of the emotional, changeable, inexperienced, immature adolescent. He is warmly affectionate and extremely curious about sex. Love is a new feeling, a first experience. To ask a young teen-ager to weigh the love-value of petting in the back seat of a car with his new girlfriend is to demand too much of him. He hardly understands love itself, is grasping to establish his own identity, and often feels bewildered by the opposite sex. To suggest that an adolescent answer an always difficult question like this is simply to expect more than his topsy-turvy world of the moment will allow him.

I said earlier that sexual intimacy could be selfish on the part of the boy or the girl or both. They could be using each other. This is especially true for the adolescent. I think, then, from a practical point of view, that we can offer the young some fairly precise norms to govern their courtship. I do not like to stress that it is a sin if you do this or do that. I would rather say, "You don't do this unless you really care for the girl or the boy. And if you go beyond these boundaries, you can normally be sure that it is not real love, but selfishness on your part. You were using her (or him)." This is true because age, emotional immaturity and a host of other factors make it exceptionally difficult for him or her to establish a deep, personal, permanent love for another partner, at least the kind that marriage requires.

Later on, in the older couple, the engaged one, the issue is not so categorical. Petting, sexual intercourse may not be selfish on either part. I would say it is better to wait, better for their love relationship and for their inner peace. But I would not say they automatically are selfish if they do not wait.

6. *There should be frank and sincere dialogue between couples in love.* We know that mutual, sincere, open discussion between a man and a woman contemplating marriage is essential. Communication must be present for a happy union and it should extend to all areas of common concern. This includes, naturally, the dilemma of premarital lovemaking and the question of how far they can go. It is enormously difficult to understand the feeling and thinking processes of the opposite sex; it is even more difficult to fathom those elements in a particular member of the opposite sex. It is not easy, then, to know what stimulates, sexually, physically, the other partner. We learn from scientific data contained in Masters and Johnson's *Human Sexual Response* and the simple directives of marriage manuals the more obvious actions which can bring on sexual arousal. But the impact upon a partner of the less evident, the more indirect gestures somewhat removed from strictly genital areas is not so clear.

One specific action arouses this girl; the same movement has little or no effect upon another. On a given night some particular gesture of affection may be tremendously exciting for the girl or the boy; on another night, it may not bother either one of them at all.

When I treat of specific points like French kissing or petting, I can draw on the experience of centuries, of past moral theologians and writers and counselors, or I can point to more modern scientific research.

But any norms as to what is so exclusive to marriage that engaged couples should not indulge in them are not the strict, absolute rules of physics and chemistry. They are more akin to the statistical rules of sociologists. They "generally" are accurate. "In most cases" they hold true. Hence we cannot apply them absolutely to each individual. Hettlinger, in another context, speaks of "the tyranny of statistics."[16] We could apply his phrase to the point at issue. For example, because many or most couples find French kissing overstimulating, it does not follow that every couple will discover this to be true.

That is precisely why so much rests upon the individual's responsibility and also why honest, mutual discussion between partners in love is imperative. As the relationship warms and deepens, they will decide some actions are just too exciting for them as a couple. Or one partner may discover a specific action is simply too stimulating for him or her personally. These will need to be postponed until marriage. The couple may find other actions, troublesome for most couples, no problem for them and a legitimate means of expressing their feelings for each other. So, too, each person needs to be honest and admit when, on a given evening, a normally nonexciting action seems charged with feeling and passion.

This sincere, mutual, frank dialogue can have value later on in married life. Sexual intercourse, through proper prelude and postlude, ideally should be a rich, satisfying experience. Actions found tremendously stimulating in courtship, but postponed and sacrificed until marriage, certainly will be remembered by the couple after they exchange nuptial vows. These same actions, recalled and relished then in the marriage bed, should prove most helpful in perfecting the couple's sexual life.

Such discussion, finally, can be helpful in a different way. I think couples should openly discuss, "How far can we go?" If they establish definite goals for themselves in a moment free from passion, then later, in a more tumultuous time, the stronger partner may sustain the weaker one. If they have agreed that they will go only this far, then later, when one, during a particular evening, feels inclined to go farther, the other may remember their previous agreement and realize that they truly don't want to give in and go on. The game of guessing is also eliminated by such dialogue. No longer does he wonder, "How far will she let me go?" or "How far does she want me to go?" No longer does she ponder, "How far does he expect me to go?" or "How far does he *really* want to go?" Each now knows. They may not live up to their goals, as we will discuss in a later chapter. But the possibilities of doing so are much better.

General Code of Conduct

The preceding background material paves the way, now, for a general norm covering the question of "How far can we go?" If this basic discussion has seemed lengthy and unnecessary, remember that I am concerned more with motivation and attitudes in young adults than with handy, packaged rules. I prefer to give young Americans tools with which to think and to make responsible judgments in this dating business. As a consequence, the actual handling of practical situations will form a relatively minor portion of this chapter.

My code is this:

When a man (woman) senses that he (she) is starting to become aroused and is getting overexcited, then it is time for him (her) to come up for air, take a breather and let the situation calm down. In addition, when one partner senses that the other is becoming aroused and getting overexcited, the partner under better control has a responsibility to come up for air, take the breather, and let the situation calm down.

How does a person know he (she) or his (her) partner is aroused? I, for one, am not about to give some sure, telltale signs. How can anyone? True, certain physical, biological reactions signify the onset of sexual stimulation and arousal. But, as mentioned, these vary from individual to individual and in individuals, from time to time. Without ducking behind vague generalities to evade the issue, I think it appropriate to say each person usually senses when, and recognizes the time to stop. Also, the frank, sincere dialogue I talked about makes it possible for one partner to understand better the "boiling point" of his or her companion.

This rule, I hope, avoids falling into the undesirable pit of "double standard" morality. Traditional principles often seem to impose total obligation of control and chastity upon a woman. The one I have just enunciated places equal responsibility upon the man and the woman.

The second sentence of the rule covers the frequently verified fact that one partner, particularly the female, becomes aroused and stimulated more slowly than the other. I do not think the undisturbed partner can so easily dismiss her (or his) responsibility simply because "I wasn't bothered at all." For example, the high school girl who necks for a long time with her boyfriend may be very happy, content and secure, without passion at all; her partner, however, may be climbing through the ceiling. Is she to be absolved of blame because her passions have remained fairly dormant?

Suggested Guidelines

I have just insisted that I would not give some sure, telltale signs that a person is overheated sexually in a dating relationship. Nevertheless the facts of biology and the experience of couples, confessors and counselors over so many years do give abundant data on what actions generally tend to arouse a person from a physically sexual point of view. These following comments, to be interpreted only as suggested guidelines, may prove of value, particularly for the perplexed younger person who seeks more definite guidance in his unsophisticated, inexperienced days than the necessarily vague direction contained in my general rule.

Hand-holding, arm around the other partner. On a given occasion nearly any physical contact can trigger a whole set of tremendously powerful sexual forces. This is true of holding hands or placing arms around each other. But those cases form the exception rather than the rule. I suppose if the individual is swimming with warm, affectionate blood, or if the boy crunches his girl with a vise-like grip, there could be some difficulties. But generally . . . no problem.

Dancing. Are West Pointers still required to dance

with daylight between partners? Americans don't any-more. Well, I take that back. I run a dozen dances a year for my high school youngsters. And at each one I feel obliged several times to apologize for walking between two kids who, supposedly, are dancing to-gether. They actually are about a dozen feet apart facing in opposite directions and doing the slip, the slop, the flip, the flop, the jerk, the monkey or some other exhausting gymnastic exercise. There is little danger that these energetic athletes will break the Sixth Commandment—"Thou shalt not commit adultery"—through their dancing. But they very well might vio-late the Fifth—"Thou shalt not kill"!

The tight, close, wrapped-up-with-each-other type of slow dancing might be a different matter. Several years ago I asked ten of our older high school students their views on this kind of thing. The group was a mix-ture of boys and girls and a balanced one at that. Some could have been classified as stereotype seminary and convent material. The others seemed to have no other interests beyond dating, dancing and the opposite sex. Yet this diversified group returned unanimous anony-mous answers. Their responses: It depends. They felt such involved dancing might be stimulating sexually to the partners or it might not be, depending on various factors — the individuals, the way it is done, the time, etc. I think their judgment was healthy and accurate.

Kissing. A kiss signifies caring. On the side of the cheek it may mean friendship; on the lips that, and usually more. There is a certain surrender contained in the kiss for a girl, a certain, remote beginning of the process leading to that ultimate giving in sexual inter-course. The kiss, obviously, can arouse more swiftly and easily than hand-holding and hugging. But the re-action is not that automatic and so much depends on the kind and intensity of kiss, the length of time the couple are kissing or "necking" and a whole host of other elements. This is an excellent illustration of my point. No one can decide how much or how many for the couple. They must make the judgment for them-selves based on the rule I have given.

What must be considered here, and especially in the case of dancing, is the inability of adults, particularly celibate ones, to judge how much kissing should be permitted or how close the dancing should be allowed. As adults we tend to see sin and stimulation where there is none; as a celibate, the priest, sister, single lay person also tends to be hypersensitive and not a qualified judge. Give the young adults sound training, true principles and let them decide.

I believe it can be wise to stress the essential goodness of a kiss when love is present. My high school students normally applaud when I mention that it is as pleasing to God for a couple to kiss properly when they really care for each other as it is for them to visit the sick. The theology may be a bit shaky, but it does get the idea across. At least I *think* I know why they are clapping!

Teen-agers wonder about a kiss on the first date. I do not feel this is a matter of morality but rather a question of personal preference. For some the simple kiss good night denotes a "thank-you" for the pleasant evening. For others, the kiss means more, something special, reserved for the person who does care, and is held back for several dates until that "special" relationship has developed.

French kissing. Like most priests I have answered questions about the rightness or wrongness of this soul or tongue kissing for many years. It is not uncommon for young adults to hear that such an intimate display of affection should be reserved for marriage and is always a "mortal sin." Father Kavanaugh painfully describes the college students' preoccupation with this dilemma. My experience has been, first of all, that some couples do not find this appealing to them. Secondly, almost all of them agree that French kissing is much more inflammatory than ordinary embracing. Finally, I have discovered that certain couples with mature emotional control can practice this without becoming overly aroused. When asked, therefore, I would respond that added caution should be used, that in itself this kind of kissing does not automatically arouse the person, and that the couple must decide for themselves according to my fundamental rule.

I find that this response proves highly satisfactory to the inquiring young mind. There is real resentment and disbelief upon the part of late high school and college students when categorically told: "French kissing is always a serious sin." They recognize the fact of potential stimulation that can arise from French kissing but they also know, often from personal experience, that it does not automatically bring this on. Thus they reject the absolute condemnation of French kissing. The questioning man or woman usually walks away content when told about the "dangers" of French kissing, the varied, but not automatic reaction it can cause, and the particular decision each must make.

It should be evident however that younger, more impressionistic and immature persons very likely should avoid this kind of kissing. They usually do not have the kind of emotional control demanded.

I do not think my approach drives scores of couples to free, guiltless French kissing. They are not all that eager to take it up. Their resentment is, I believe, based on how and what we say about the topic. A categorical rejection simply does not fit the facts in their minds and smacks of the legalistic morality Father Kavanaugh decries. The explanation I have offered does fit the facts, from many points of view, and they accept that.

In support of my position, in passing, I would like to note that one of the manuals of moral theology employed by many older parish priests in America admits the possibility that French kissing is not always a serious offense. Father Heribert Jone comments, "So also is tongue-kissing (or soul kissing) usually seriously sinful."[17] The moral theologian takes a more severe approach than I do, but does say "usually" not "always," thus admitting the possibility of variations for individuals. Hence even an old-school moralist writing in dry, legal terms would not condone the advice of the clergyman who categorically condemns French kissing as always a serious sin.

Light petting. Couples use this phrase generally to cover light touches of the body over the clothing, particularly of the breast. In terms of the principles I have maintained, reserving for marriage sexual intercourse and those things which closely lead up to it, I advise couples to try to avoid this kind of light petting. The reasons are mainly physical ones, substantiated by the book *Human Sexual Response* and the testimony of several physician-specialists I consulted. Contrary to French kissing, there *is* an automatic reaction when the woman's breasts are caressed. The presence of erectile tissue, the enlargement of the breast during excitation, the experiential fact that a woman senses this through her whole body, the deep satisfaction she receives through such fondling (often as satisfying to her as sexual intercourse) — these confirm the almost necessary arousal which follows from even light petting. It also, much more so than French kissing, tends to set in progress a pattern that in time culminates and attains satisfaction in sexual intercourse.

I do then, when asked, counsel couples for their own peace to stop short of light petting. I would say, on balance, that many, if not most couples feel this is the best policy. This is the goal they set for themselves. How faithful they remain to that goal is a different question.

Heavy or deep petting. Couples usually lump under this phrase very extensive, involved touches, particularly of the genitals, often resulting in orgasm. More simply, it seems to include everything beyond light petting short of sexual intercourse. From what I have just said relative to light petting, it should be evident that I advise couples also to try and avoid this type of heavy petting. If light petting arouses and sets in motion the intricate and powerful process leading to sexual intercourse, it follows that deep, heavy petting does so to an even greater degree.

* * * *

This chapter may be the most concrete, practical one of the book. It might be the first read and most interesting for young readers. But it is the least important. The value of proper motivation far outweighs the importance of pragmatic rules. I return, therefore, in the next section to that more significant issue—the why of premarital chastity as discussed by several young adults presently struggling with the challenge.

7. *The New Generation*

$p$rophets of gloom feel that today's youth and tomorrow's adults possess precious little idealism, courage or generosity. In fact they seem to think that the new generation lacks practically every positive quality supposedly so prevalent in the "good old days." I do not share that view. My experience with the young indicates the vast majority of them are serious, concerned about other people, anxious to attack today's problems, extremely idealistic and courageous in a good cause. But to sense and appreciate this you must be close to them, gain their confidence, and listen. Especially listen. They have something to tell us — about sex and love and chastity, as well as about all the other great issues in life.

In preparing this book, I sought the help of some college students. After all, the challenges of courtship and chastity do touch them most directly. Sex, religion and politics used to be, in my campus days, the great topics of conversation. I presume time has not altered the agenda too much. It seemed to me that student reflections and comments could be of valuable assistance.

Questionnaires were distributed to approximately 60 seniors in an all-girl college and to a similar number of senior boys in a coeducational university. The question posed was: "If you really love this boy (or girl), then why isn't it permissible to make love, pet, even go all the way?"

The students were all, or at least nearly all, Roman Catholics. An explanation of the question further noted that my interest was not in the response, "The Church says so, It's against the Sixth Commandment, It's a mortal sin, etc.," but in a reply that would give different motivational reasons in behalf of premarital chastity. I was seeking deep, honest reasons why they felt the love between a couple, engaged or truly in love, would be strengthened by a chaste, controlled courtship as opposed to a courtship in which there are little, if any, limitations placed on the sexual expression of this mutual love. It was further mentioned that such motivation might be helpful to couples in their age bracket who are struggling to control feelings and find simple, negative warnings or commands not always sufficient to meet the challenge.

A sample reason was offered as an illustration. A young woman in one of my marriage classes had remarked the previous year, "It takes love to keep going when you are with your boyfriend; but it takes more love to stop."

Anonymity was assured and sought in the survey; honesty of response desired above all. Unfortunately, this writer has no professional competence in developing that kind of questionnaire. Consequently, the question as stated actually seeks an answer in support of the position presented in this book. Those who opposed my philosophy or disagreed with the statement very likely would have hesitated to respond for a variety of reasons. The response was limited — 20 percent of the girls and 10 percent of the boys returned the forms in the stamped, self-addressed envelope provided.

I admit the weakness involved in my procedure and intend to prove nothing through the responses. They are, however, extremely frank and they offer, I believe, significant and at times even magnificent insights. The replies picked for inclusion in this chapter were selected as the best by an above average high school student and a widely read young man.

A. The Male Response

Response Number 1:

It was six months after I met Sue when we decided that we were in love with each other. That was two years ago. And we believe that to control ourselves for such a long period of time has been nothing less than a miracle. But the real reason we have remained fairly chaste is because we are both strongly ethical people. Once we knew we were in love we talked, sometimes at great length, about sex and sexual relationships. We both believe that ignoring the problem would not take it away. We found that saying no to ourselves individually and while with each other was the real clue to happiness. We recognized early that for two ethical people to suspend all prior attitudes toward chastity would be very hypocritical. Thus we set out from the very beginning to maintain a reasonably healthy approach to the problem. True, we have had our moments. But always, before something serious would happen, we would cut it off.

Really, though, we think engaging in sexual acts would cheapen us in each other's eyes, and God forbid that either of us should feel that way. When two people love each other, they have a respect not so much of themselves, but more in the line with respect of the other, *and* the fulfillment of a true and everlasting relationship. And what relationship that began with sex and which focused on sex has ever lasted more than a few years, or brought the happiness and security the two people thought it would bring? Lasting happiness does not begin in a parked car or a bedroom, but in the hearts of each other. And to base a relationship on sex and not love is a misfortune to both parties. Sacrifice is the key to happiness, not only now, but after marriage as well. Once a friend of mine said, "I can't wait to get married, then I can get it 'all the time.' " Afterward I thought to myself how ignorant he was because he didn't have enough insight to realize that he isn't going to get "it all the time," for various reasons, health being one of them.

Sue and I could sit for hours (and we've done it) and simply talk about things, some trivial, some intellectual, but all very important. It is important to meet the other in the mind and heart, not in a boudoir. We know that if two people can be as compatible as we are, then it is unnecessary to try the shoe on before buying it, as the saying goes. Two people who find each other so fascinating with clothes on, will undoubtedly find themselves just as fascinating with them off. *We can wait!* And we will, because we recognize that sex is not the most important thing in a marriage, although it is a large part; it is love, cherishing, respect, and sacrifice. All these things must come first if a lasting relationship is to develop. That is why we can wait. Every bit we sacrifice now will gain us strength to sacrifice later. And we are not so naive as to think that since we're going to get married anyway, it is all right to commit the act now. We know that adding sex to our relationship would only make us look for other things, things which will not do us any good now, for almost always they end up in unwed mothers . . . and two broken hearts.

Response Number 2:

In response to your letter, perhaps the following observations would be helpful. I view the sex act as one of the most perfect ways in which two persons can express their love. However, I question both the sincerity and the depth of the relationship of two persons whose chief criterion for love is sexual compatibility. Charles Schulz has a Peanuts book out entitled *Love Is Holding Hands*. This expresses better than I ever could what I feel love is. "Love is just sitting there together, not talking but merely enjoying each other's presence"; "Love is a special song or a favorite poem"; "Love is walking hand in hand around Blue Lake or taking long drives in the country"; etc. I could go on for quite a long time, but I'll spare you the agony.

Of course I'd be lying if I said that sex didn't enter into my relations with my girl. I feel that it is a large and a GOOD part of our love—even the occasional petting. I'm sorry if that's not what you want to hear, but I can only write what I feel is true. We have never been to bed together, though we came pretty close once. It was a horrible feeling believe me; one I never hope to experience again. That's the one thing I really can't figure out. You love someone and you express your love physically, yet as your relationship deepens so do the physical manifestations, and it all seems so natural; there is nothing dirty or sordid about it; nothing which I am ashamed of. Yet, when you go out with a girl you know just as a social acquaintance and get some sex off her, you, or at least I, have a bit of a guilty and ashamed feeling afterward. This all points to some sort of a difference which I feel can be illustrated by our society. All our relationships, or at least most of them, seem to be governed by our viewing others as functions rather than persons. If all a fellow cares about in a relationship is sex, then he has depersonalized his girlfriend and the relationship. However, if sex is merely a part of a fuller whole, then the girl is a person and "thou," rather than a body and an "it."

Well, that's about it. It's all yours to sift through. I'm sorry I haven't been able to lay down any moral dogmas. The only one I feel qualified to talk for is myself and my only source is my own experience. I would like to claim credit for the philosophical insights, but unfortunately they belong to my ethics professor and Martin Buber, respectively. I also feel that my girl being over in Europe for the year has made me look at our relationship from a different angle than I would have if she were here.

Thank you for giving me the opportunity to set down on paper the thoughts that have been collecting for so long in my mind. While you offer "complete anonymity" I would like to give my name and address as well as an offer of whatever future assistance I can render. Books like this are always needed. However, to be accepted by all, they must speak to us, not preach at us and put more moral limitations on us.

I wish you all the luck in your work.

Note: The following reply came from a girl's college. Apparently the young woman had written her boyfriend and copied his hastily composed but valuable commentary before adding her own remarks.

Response Number 3:
"Pregnancy . . . a hasty marriage (or one earlier than planned) . . . the suspicion that if a girl would bed down with you, there might have been others, possibly reflecting poorly on her character and on her outlook on sex in general. It also tends to induce guilt feelings (more in girls, I guess) about what happened which they might transfer over to the guy as the "reason" for such feelings, eventually souring the relationship entirely. I put reason in because it takes two to tangle. I don't think it would be fair for the

guy to take advantage of the girl if he knew that, upon sober reflection, she would regret her giving in (even if she wasn't pregnant). If you are going to sleep with someone, then do it, but it shouldn't be the hide-in-a-motel-so-no-one-will-know type of thing. It requires a total commitment of both parties, in or out of marriage; and that is not something that can be given generally before marriage."

My boyfriend

* * * *

I honestly feel that sex and intercourse are such beautiful things, it isn't right to make them something that is done on the sly. After making love, one shouldn't have guilt feelings . . . they should remember the occasion as one of the more beautiful times in their life. That is possible, I think, only if the people involved are married to each other.

I think I would feel funny if I knew my husband had made love with some other girl. I think I would wonder if he enjoyed it more with her than with me. By the same token, I feel the greatest gift a girl can give her husband is the gift of virginity.

Marriage should be something to look forward to, not something that is forced upon you because of pregnancy. Why get married if you already are doing something which is supposedly only for marriage?

B. The Female Response
Response Number 1:

I have found that sexual expression in a love relationship eventually ruins a beautiful thing. You love someone and you *respect* him. This is important to me, anyway. You get intimate and involved in sexual play and for some reason, the love isn't as beautiful anymore. You hate yourself because you have drawn him into sin. You love this boy, but you'd take away his perfect happiness. You would send him to hell! And then you begin to think the same thing of him. If he really loved you, he'd want you to have everlasting happiness.

The fiancé of one of our classmates was killed not long ago. I think, What if it had been my fiancé? If we had been fooling around with premarital sex and he had been killed the next night, how would I feel?

Live for today—don't think of the past or future. Die today and die happily and leave your loved one behind with a mind at peace. I hate to sound so morbid, but with death so close, it does make a deep impression.

If you have a relationship based on sex, I feel sorry for you (the engaged couple). What will you have when you're 20 years older? You are missing something truly wonderful — knowing the whole person. Something you'll never forget. There will be other bodies.

Find and cherish the wonderfully unique person you love. Love him, don't make love to him. It spoils everything. I know. And I regret it so much. We got caught up with each other's bodies and forgot about the minds, the ambitions, the wonders. We lived in the present—the material, pleasurable present. What love could have been if we could have lived for the past, present and future—for complete memories, without regrets ripping at our minds. Without tears trying to wash away the shroud of death of love we had enrobed ourselves in.

You may find you tire of each other. You end up the same way night after night. It must get monotonous, don't you think? Your body tingles and grasps for your love's, but love slips from your grasp when you release it from its foremost situation and replace it with a tangible.

Please don't ruin your love. It's hard, but you show more love by self-control than by reckless, selfish grabbing.

Father, please pray for me, that a love that has been eroded may be refertilized. Thank you!

Response Number 2:

I am presently engaged to a boy I have gone with since my junior year in high school. I really don't think my reply could be used in your book as it does not stress a chaste courtship, but perhaps I could be used as a negative example, or I may say something that will give you some insights into where I have gone wrong. In any case, this will be honest.

I have gone steady with my boyfriend since my

junior year in high school. Things started out very well — in fact, he never even kissed me until we had gone together for about a month. In senior year and his first year in college we used to make out, but that was all — no petting. He was studying drafting and did very well, but was advised to go into the service and go to school while in the service. Then when he got out, one more year of school and he would have his degree and the service would be behind him. Well, it was when he came home on leave after seven months of separation that he first touched me and that was all we did — touch each other. The same thing happened when he came home before he went away — this time for 18 months. He says he would never make love to me because he knows the hurt and shame I would feel afterward, and if he can't protect me from himself, how can he protect me from others. Father, I really love him and I know he loves me because we have been apart (in miles) for a long stretch of time but always close in spirit. If anything, being apart I think has helped us to realize how much we love each other. In April we will be married and I hope we will have a happy marriage. He is a non-Catholic, but when we first started going together I explained that our children had to be brought up Catholic. Lately he has hinted at converting (I hope he does, but I'm not pushing!).

I know petting is wrong, Father, but honestly when he touches me I am so happy. When I go to confession I tell the priest exactly what happened. I am sorry, but yet happy in a way. Somehow I have the feeling that God understands me in a special way. Maybe that is what you would call rationalizing.

Response Number 3:

I suppose since my fiancé and I have not remained chaste, that this should make it easier for me to answer. Actually, it isn't for some unknown reason.

Although I have not remained pure, I must say that young couples should. Not for God, their parents, or society, but for themselves. It really makes a great difference in their relationship. Trying not to give in rather than to do it proves the strength of your own character and gives one the satisfaction of saving one-self for the one you love. No matter how much in love you are, you cannot always be sure that the two of you will get married. There's no guarantee. You and he are the ones who have to live with yourselves. Guilt feelings are aroused and you also wonder if he really loves you for what you are or for what you are giving him. And even if he tells you he loves you, there's always a shade of doubt. I know, believe me. This leads to a vague distrust which sooner or later builds a wall between the couple. Selfishness creeps in subtly.

God has nearly nothing to do with a decision of being chaste. It is generally the thought of society, social pressure, and how this would affect this society and your parents, relatives and friends.

Sex is beautiful, but it can become ugly and gross if used in a wrong way. A fear of it may develop if it is also carried out in the back seat of a car, or a motel, where you are conscious that someone may find you out or catch you. Then it loses its beauty. This in itself could ruin a very wonderful relationship and love between a couple. Respect may be lost even though it is not shown or even expressed.

Premarital sex takes trust, love and respect from a relationship and these are necessary to endure the ups and downs of living with a husband and family.

Something is missing from the marriage, even though premarital relations are with the guy you marry. (I've seen it in a marriage.)

It's very difficult to give an exact answer because there are so many and such individualistic circumstances.

I realize too late what I should have done in the first place, but like a monkey I wanted security and thought this to be the way. The only advice I can give is try as hard as you can not to give in; it has its rewards. It truly does take more love to stop than to keep going.

Response Number 4:

Presently I am going with a boy quite seriously, and although we are not engaged, we do intend marriage in the near future. And believe me, we are having a real hard time "behaving ourselves." I thank God that we are both Catholic and have the strength of our religion to keep us on the right road. But honestly, when we are tempted to go farther than we should, it is *not* the fact that it's a mortal sin that stops us. Not at the exact moment of "decision" anyway. It's more of a selfish one — for five minutes of pleasure we would completely ruin everything we have worked so hard for. We both contemplate graduation this coming June, and both hope to go on to school, he for a master's in chemistry and myself for one in education. All these hopes and plans would be abolished if we both had to quit school now to get married because we let our hearts run away with our heads!

We also consider our parents. They are four outstanding adults, spiritual'y, personally, and socially. I can think of no better way of hurting them than by giving into temptation.

Those are our reasons, Father. Selfish? Maybe. Not based on the Church's teaching? Maybe. But those are facts. Tangible facts. Ones that have meaning to us — and they've worked. And I pray to God they continue to do so.

Thank you for even considering our opinion.

8. Starting Over

*M*y seminary training, typical for those times, was very, very cut and dried. There were neat, clear, clean compartments in which to place the problems of human life we soon would face. Tightly logical arguments, ageless and unswerving moral principles, definite dogmas, tried and true solutions—these gave us a veritable arsenal of ammunition with which to attack the forces of evil. Armed with this impressive array of weapons, I charged forth from the cathedral sanctuary on ordination day ready and willing to solve all difficulties, answer all questions, convert all sinners, change the entire world.

Life is full of rude awakenings.

Mine began the first day in parish work.

I found that life was a bit more complicated than the picture of it I had visualized in the seminary. A seemingly infinite number of factors affect the way people act. Discouragement can so depress and weaken us that we do things we ordinarily would never do. The passion of hate, anger, lust can cloud our vision and lead us astray. That vague, mysterious, all-encompassing characteristic known as weakness frequently plays its part. Some persons are impetuous, others are overly curious, still others struggle along with exceptionally strong sex drives. The pace and pressure of the business world build tensions and worry, leading men to seek some sort of relief, and not always in legitimate ways. The heart of man also is restless at times, not content with peace, curiously craving for some excitement, some change from the frequent boredom within him. It is all so complex, so difficult to weigh the numerous, varying and individual circumstances which surround every man.

All of this does not deny the value of the seminary training and the truths taught in its classrooms. It is, rather, a further testimony to the difficulty in adjusting from the theoretical, idea-heavy atmosphere of the collegiate campus to the concrete, practical problems of the real world. As priests, we are not alone. The doctor, lawyer, teacher suffers the same painful experience. There are false starts and embarrassing mistakes. Unusual is the person who is wise and experienced without passing through the crucible of beginning failures. Years of work with people should make a priest wiser, more sympathetic, more understanding. I hope a dozen years at a busy, downtown parish, exposed to all that is good and bad, great and terrible in man, has mellowed me.

Life seems to be a combination of lofty ideals and human failures. We need and want to aim for the sky. But we also need to prepare ourselves for setbacks. So in this book. The previous chapters have attempted to establish extremely high standards in the sexual realm. Some readers, I know, will consider them impractical or unattainable. But I push on, calling readers to view sex as sublime and to set norms governing sexual behavior accordingly. Still, flesh and blood does not always live up to these great expectations. The last chapter offered poignant illustrations of the stress and strain, the ups and downs of striving for premarital chastity. This one deals with the weakness of man, his lapses from established goals, his renewed efforts to live according to principles that he has established for himself.

Weakness

We should not be surprised. The lessons of history and the teachings of God and men speak to us about human nature's weakness.

The night before he died, Jesus himself needed the comfort and support of companionship. He looked for it from his closest associates. They failed him. He knew and yet understood this, their failure.

> "Then Jesus went with them to a place called Gethsemane, and he said to his disciples, 'Sit here, while I go yonder and pray.' And taking with him Peter and the two sons of Zebedee, he began to be sorrowful and troubled. Then he said to them, 'My soul is very sorrowful and troubled, even to death; remain here, and watch with me.' And going a little farther he fell on his face and

prayed, 'My Father, if it be possible, let this cup pass from me; nevertheless, not as I will, but as thou wilt.' And he came to the disciples and found them sleeping; and he said to Peter, 'So, could you not watch with me one hour? Watch and pray that you may not enter into temptation; the spirit indeed is willing, but the flesh is weak' " (Matt. 26:36-41).[1]

It was hardly malice upon the part of the three Apostles. Weakness is the better word. The parallel between this and the young couple, deeply in love, with noble goals, yet stumbling on occasion from their high standards, is obvious. Willing spirits, but weak flesh.

Only a few years later, St. Paul sketched this inner struggle which every man faces.

"I do not understand my own actions. For I do not do what I want, but I do the very thing I hate. Now if I do what I do not want, I agree that the law is good. So then it is no longer I that do it, but sin which dwells within me. For I know that nothing good dwells within me, that is, in my flesh. I can will what is right, but I cannot do it. For I do not do the good I want, but the evil I do not want is what I do. Now if I do what I do not want, it is no longer I that do it, but sin which dwells within me.

"So I find it to be a law that when I want to do right, evil lies close at hand. For I delight in the law of God, in my inmost self, but I see in my members another law at war with the law of my mind and making me captive to the law of sin which dwells in my members. Wretched man that I am! Who will deliver me from this body of death? Thanks be to God through Jesus Christ our Lord" (Rom. 7:15-25).[2]

The Catholic Church shares this acceptance of man's weakness and shows it on many occasions. The funeral rite is one example. The officiating priest meets the body at the door of the church. He sprinkles the casket with blessed water, recites Psalm 129 begging for the forgiveness of the Lord and then reads the following prayer:

"O Lord, we commend to you the soul of your servant, that, having departed from this world, he (she) may live with you. And by the grace of your merciful love, wash away the sins that in human frailty he (she) has committed in the conduct of his (her) life."[3]

How much the word human frailty includes — broken promises, momentary or lengthy lapses from the path of virtue, slight and serious failures in honesty, temperance, sex. There are indeed people whose lives reflect a steady and strong pattern of rejection of every temptation. These are saints with courage. But most of us are sinners with weakness.

The modern mass communications media offer ample witness to this. The newspaper carries daily stories of human weakness. Today's novels and movies often take as the central theme the inner conflict of man, the war between his higher and lower self. Dr. Zhivago, torn between a beautiful, adoring wife and an equally beautiful and loving mistress, presents a graphic picture of this struggle. His weakness and, even more, the many involuntary events which complicate his life prompted a number of high school students discussing the film to feel very sympathetically about his plight and to wonder just how severely God would judge the Russian doctor.

That basic weakness in man touches all areas of his life and the sexual aspect is no exception. In contemporary civilization, however, the struggle for sexual control is tremendously intensified by cultural pressures and factors. A whole complex of diverse elements conspires to make it difficult for the young man and woman. Harvey Cox, in the chapter we have quoted earlier, examines with great insight these various points. Sex is used to sell products of every kind. Why not use sex simply for pleasure, as a thing, divorced from connection with a person? Cars, motel, the empty home are easily made available to adolescents. The opportunity is there, why not use it? Films and television tend to be heavily sex centered. Besides falsely identifying sex and love, such visual demonstrations naturally arouse a boy and a girl's curiosity and desire. A spirit of general freedom, sophisticated arguments in favor of free love, the style of dress, the amount of leisure time, the delay of marriage by educational needs—the list is endless. Our only point here is to stress that in addition to the fundamental weakness in man, the prevalent attitude and cultural environment make chastity even more difficult.

Michael Kind, as a young man in 1939, shared both this human weakness and these modern pressures. After his dismal experience with the two "pigs" in Maury's apartment, he promised that he would have no sex until he fell in love.

"It was five months before he broke his vow of chastity. Accompanying Maury to a *bar mitzvah* in Hartford — the *bar mitzvah* of Maury's brother-in-law's sister's son — he met the sister of the confirmee, a slim girl with black hair and very smooth white skin and thin, waxy nostrils. When they danced at the party that evening he noticed that her hair smelled sweet and clean, like soapy water that had dried in the sun. The two of them left the house and he drove Maury's Plymouth into a country road off the Wilbur Cross Parkway. He pulled the car under a huge chestnut tree whose lowest branches brushed the car roof and they kissed a lot until things happened without plot or plan. Afterward, sharing a cigarette, he told her that he had broken a promise to himself that this would never happen again until it was with a girl he loved.

"He expected her to laugh but the girl seemed to think this was very sad. 'You mean it?' she said. 'Really?'

" 'Really. And I don't love you,' he said, adding hastily, 'how could I? I mean, I hardly know you.'

" 'I don't love you either. But I like you a lot,' she said. 'Won't that do?' They both agreed it was the next best thing."[4]

Courage

There certainly are those who question the desirability or even possibility of premarital chastity. But few would cavil about the courage needed to practice it. The norms seem astronomically high, hardly suited for the complacent, the soft, the self-indulgent. Only a strong, determined, industrious, courageous person could ever resist the pull of weak human nature and modern society in this matter. We are talking here about control of feelings, direction of our drives. Sex is pleasurable; everybody, apparently, is doing it; I deeply love this girl or boy and feel an almost compelling desire to express it, to succumb or surrender. To follow the norms of this book surely demands effort, strength and, ultimately, courage to follow one's principles regardless of opposition from within or from without.

The late President John F. Kennedy admired courage and courageous men. He opened his book, *Profiles in Courage,* with this sentence: "This is a book about that most admirable of human virtues—courage."[5] His close brother, Senator Robert F. Kennedy, has written a "foreword to the Memorial Edition" which offers some further insight into the man and his thinking.

> "Courage is the virtue that President Kennedy most admired. He sought out those people who had demonstrated in some way, whether it was on a battlefield or a baseball diamond, in a speech or fighting for a cause, that they had courage, that they would stand up, that they could be counted on.
>
> "That is why this book so fitted his personality, his beliefs. It is a study of men who, at risk to themselves, their futures, even the well-being of their children, stood fast for principles. It was toward that ideal that he modeled his life. And this in time gave heart to others.
>
> "As Andrew Jackson said, 'One man with courage makes a majority.' That is the effect President Kennedy had on others.
>
> "President Kennedy would have been forty-seven in May of 1964. At least one half of the days that he spent on this earth were days of in-

tense physical pain. He had scarlet fever when he was very young, and serious back trouble when he was older. In between he had almost every other conceivable ailment. When we were growing up together we used to laugh about the great risk a mosquito took in biting Jack Kennedy — with some of his blood the mosquito was almost sure to die. He was in Chelsea Naval Hospital for an extended period of time after the war, had a major and painful operation on his back in 1955, campaigned on crutches in 1958. In 1951 on a trip we took around the world he became ill. We flew to the military hospital in Okinawa and he had a temperature of over 106 degrees. They didn't think he would live.

"But during all this time, I never heard him complain. I never heard him say anything that would indicate that he felt God had dealt with him unjustly. Those who knew him well would know he was suffering only because his face was a little whiter, the lines around his eyes a little deeper, his words a little sharper. Those who did not know him well detected nothing.

"He didn't complain about his problem, so why should I complain about mine — that is how one always felt. . .

"He was demonstrating conviction, courage, a desire to help others who needed help, and true and genuine love for his country."[6]

The book itself was simply dedicated, "To My Wife." Little did he dream that a final chapter could be added to *Profiles in Courage*. The courage of his wife, Jacqueline, in those dark days of tragedy, bearing with supreme dignity and grace the grief of death and separation, controlling her tears and feelings, was seen by millions of people all over the world. It has sustained others in moments of sorrow.

I would like to think that the example of this courageous man and woman might give needed courage to some young men or women struggling with weakness.

Growth Through Failure

We could divide the failures of man into two groups, permanent mistakes and temporary ones. In the permanent setbacks we give up, fail to draw any profit from them, yield entirely to self-pity, refuse to forgive ourselves, reject totally the possibility of mercy and forgiveness from God. The permanence of our failure is measured not so much by its objective seriousness as by our consequent reaction to the lapse.

In the temporary failures, we do learn, we move on, we do not give up, we forgive ourselves and others, we accept the always available mercy of a forgiving Lord. The mistake in itself may be monumental, harmful to the lives of many, and seriously detrimental to our own personal future. But as long as we are able to rise above it, then the failure is not permanent. The course of history repeatedly illustrates the principle that some good can and usually does come from our evil actions or our mistakes or the tragedies of life. Countless modern inventions were practically accidents. A false start, a careless calculation inadvertently led the inventor into an area undreamed of before the supposedly drastic error.

An advertisement in the November, 1966, issue of *Ebony* magazine confirms these statements by way of a specific example. The Old Taylor Distillery Company, promoting its Kentucky Straight Bourbon, is currently running a series on "Ingenious Americans." Number two in the set features Garrett A. Morgan (1877-1963). The full-page display contains a large, sketched portrait of the inventor with this caption in boldface type beneath it. "It took a disaster to prove his invention." The text of the advertisement develops that point:

"On July 25, 1916, a tunnel explosion trapped over twenty men working 228 feet below Lake Erie. The huge clouds of smoke, gases, dust and debris made it impossible for anyone to search for survivors. Just as it seemed hopeless, someone remembered hearing about a man named Morgan and his invention. It seemed Garrett A. Morgan had been trying to interest Ohio manufacturers in his device for a long time. It was the 'gas inhalator,' or gas mask, as we know it today.

"Morgan was summoned and quickly arrived with his brother and two gas inhalators. Together they descended into the suffocating blackness. The crowd waited silently at the surface. Could anyone penetrate the smoke and gas and come out alive? Finally, Morgan emerged carrying a survivor. Again and again he returned to the hole until he had saved over a score of workmen. This remarkable feat not only drew publicity to his invention, but marked him a hero as well.

"Morgan didn't stop there. In 1923 he patented another device — one that may annoy us at times, but has undoubtedly saved many lives —the electric stoplight. He sold the rights to a large corporation."[7]

The explosion was a black, dark tragedy for many people. But all was not lost. Some were saved that very day. And an invention was proved and publicized that in the years following surely has and will save many more. We can see the same pattern of victory through defeat, growth through failure, in our personal lives. A commonly quoted assertion in theology and philosophy maintains that God does not will sin and failure, but he can and does bring good out of our moral collapses. This is verified in a young man or woman's efforts to achieve sexual maturity.

Let's consider the example of a girl named Mary. She comes from a good home and has studied for a large part of her young life in Catholic schools. The beauty of sexual purity has been drummed into her ears; the ugliness of sexual impurity, constantly stressed. She rebels a little at the overemphasis, yet inwardly accepts the goal of chastity. In fact, she disapproves and looks down her nose at those poor "fallen girls," those who have a reputation, who are known to be loose with their boyfriends, or who have gotten into trouble. "How stupid!" she thinks to herself. "I would never do those things!" Mary self-righteously asserts to her friends.

Mary starts to date, casually at first, then steadily, then seriously. A man loves her and tells her so. She loves him and tells him so. They kiss, and kiss, and kiss some more. All that was black and bad about sex seems untrue. She finds it pleasant to be held in a man's arms, beautiful to be wanted, tender and intimate to be so close. If it is so wonderful, why is it wrong? So she increasingly wonders after each date. Finally, varied circumstances combine to present just the right situation. She surrenders. The first time she somehow manages to stop at heavy petting. But she is getting more deeply involved each time, a bit more anxious, confusedly worried. The right occasion and mood come again and Mary this time gives herself entirely.

After her date has left and she is home alone, perhaps even before in his company, there are tears. Sleep comes hard that night. A tormented conscience the next day does not give her much rest either. Eventually, usually the next day, the next Saturday, the next month or year even, the issue comes to a head or at least Mary comes to grips with it. She summons courage and visits an understanding priest and pours out her heart.

Was it a permanent or a temporary setback for Mary? It depends upon her reaction. But it can easily be merely a temporary regression on the way to sexual maturity. If her heart is now softer, more humble, more understanding of the weakness of others; if she no longer despises those so-called "fallen girls"; if her wrongful pride and self-righteousness have disappeared; if she is not so critical of others and their mistakes; if she now understands that people often do things they really didn't want to do because of weakness, confusion, loneliness, discouragement; if she is now a warmer, more forgiving individual — then Mary's lapse was serious, but only temporary, even though scars there may never be removed.

I think it is a mark of some saints and holy persons that this understanding of human weakness, this warm, patient forgiveness, this humble and noncondescending view of sinners came without actual sin and failure. Most of us, unfortunately, seem to acquire these noble attitudes only through personal lapses.

At any rate, Mary is no longer a virgin. She cannot offer her virginity at the nuptial altar either to God or to her husband. That is regrettable. But all is not lost. She does bring a deeper kindness and understanding of others. She is a warmer person now, more forgiving. In a word, she really loves all people more.

> " 'Teacher, which is the great commandment in the law?' And he said to him, 'You shall love the Lord your God with all your heart, and with all your soul, and with all your mind. This is the great and first commandment. And a second is like it, You shall love your neighbor as yourself' " (Matt. 22:36-39).
>
> "So faith, hope, love abide, these three; but the greatest of these is love" (1 Cor. 13:13).[8]

Forgive Yourself

When Rabbi Michael Kind first kissed Leslie Rawlings their relationship was a mixed one. He was, to her, more a rabbi and less a prospective boyfriend, lover, fiancé, husband. In fact, because of their religious differences, she entertained little thought that the friendly picnic and quick kiss were anything more than a casual situation. Pleasant enough, but not permanent. This led Leslie to unburden her guilt feelings about that first sexual experience at Wellesley. She confided in Michael as a rabbi, a counselor, a man who is supposed to understand these things, and listen to people, and somehow help them out of their troubles. He responded well.

> " 'I apologize,' she said. 'I wanted to tell somebody about that ever since it happened. I grew so disgusted with myself afterwards, and so sorry that I had let my curiosity get the better of me.'
>
> " 'You shouldn't let that single experience make a great big difference in your life,' he said carefully. . .
>
> " 'I don't intend to,' she said in a low voice.
>
> " 'None of us can go through life untouched. We all hurt ourselves and others. We feel boredom and we put a small creature on a hook, we

feel hunger and we eat flesh, we feel desire and we make love.'

"The girl burst into tears.

"He turned to look at her, touched and amazed that his words should have so profound an effect, but she was staring at his head as she wept."[9]

To profit from a failure, probably the most important requirement is self-forgiveness. Unless we accept ourselves as we are with both strong and weak points, successes and mistakes, we will spend the rest of our lives constantly rehashing the past, brooding over our boners, giving in to morbid self-pity, and staying depressed through excessive attention to guilt feelings. This is not self-acceptance, nor is it healthy self-love. We must move on. To do so takes effort and concentration. A few practical tips might help.

(a) *Don't make excuses for failure.* This is escapism at its worst. When we try to blame other people or other factors we simply are not facing reality. It is only superficial self-acceptance and ultimately it will crumble. We must be absolutely honest, admit sincerely we have erred, forgive ourselves, and then forget it. Digging up dead bones benefits no one.

(b) *Learn from a mistake.* It is very likely that a lapse was partially or even totally influenced by certain outside forces. Objective examination of the situation can be productive in revealing them. The following are not uncommon factors leading couples astray when deep down they really did not want to be.

Drinking. Premarital chastity is hard enough when both parties are thinking clearly and feeling normally. The overly enthused or even totally relaxed atmosphere created by some drinking may prove too much for the affectionate man and woman struggling to control their feelings until later on in marriage.

Too late at night. Dating is by its nature a rather exciting business. We enjoy one another and the entertainment. We may even be flushed with happiness over the evening. But as the night moves along, almost without realization we gradually tire. And a tired body means a weary will. Many couples regretfully remark they did things late at night they simply would not have considered doing during the day when their thinking, feeling, willing powers were at normal standards of operation.

Depression or loneliness. An engaged couple, together at the end of the week after a mutually frustrating five days of work or school, may feel an exceptionally strong impulse to seek from one another physical comfort and relief. So, too, the couple making up after a serious disagreement frequently sense an unusually compelling drive to express physically to each other their apology for the argument. In addition, the depressed or lonely individual, unable to adjust in a mature way to the tensions of work, home, school, or life in general, may, as we know, seek security and escape in sex. The person or couple can learn from these things and thus be on guard the next time a similar situation or mood seems to be setting in.

No place to go. The boyfriend who comes to his date's home with no plan for the evening hardly manifests a masculine ability to lead or thoughtful concern about showing his girl a pleasant time. In addition, the couple with a night ahead and no planned activities can slip easily into the way of least resistance. The idle mind gravitates with ease to the physical and sexual. The couple in love with some definite idea on a date of where and when and with whom may find less temptation in their way, and less tension, too.

Too long alone. Being alone is not bad. Lovers want this, and not just to kiss and make out. They share secrets, dream dreams, talk for hours. These are good things, absolutely essential for a successful engagement. But they usually discover, in time, that too much aloneness or a too-isolated separation from others may cause their situation to get out of hand more than they wish.

Jesus' words to the woman taken in adultery have meaning at this point. "Neither do I condemn you; go, and do not sin again" (John 8:11).[10] He forgave the embarrassed lady, but expected her to profit in a practical way from those mistakes. The modern young man and woman should also profit from theirs.

What I really am trying to combine are lofty goals of sexual conduct with a practical admission of the difficulties involved. This means aiming high, but calmly, humbly, honestly accepting occasional, even repeated failures. Torturing yourself with guilt feelings can often mean more self-pity and injured pride than grief over the offense committed against God or neighbor. There is no peace from exaggerated introspection. The person with self-acceptance and self-forgiveness starts over, finds his way back, begins again. As Father Capon mentioned, a tardy dose of principle is better than none at all.

Telling the Next Partner

A brief while back a young woman in great distress came to see me. She had been engaged several years ago and had committed several indiscretions with her fiancé. Eventually the engagement was broken, the couple drifted apart, and went their separate ways. Now in love and engaged to another man, she wonders what to tell him. Their relationship has been warm, but chaste. Should she admit she is no longer a virgin and tell of her affair with the first man? Will he still accept her, or think less of her, or even reject her? Or should she remain silent?

She was not the first young woman to come, nor, I presume, will she be the last to seek some assistance in resolving this dilemma.

Ultimately, of course, she alone can make the decision. She knows him, the situation, all the circumstances surrounding her past behavior and the present courtship. In seeking advice from the priest, this girl wanted either guidance from a person outside the present case, presumably one with experience in handling such difficulties, or she simply wished support for a decision she had already though hesitatingly reached.

The young woman can be given one certain bit of advice. Concern over the loss of virginity in a strictly physical sense of the term need not be a source of undue anxiety. Medical science makes it clear that the hymen can be fractured in a variety of ways other than through sexual intercourse. Therefore, her husband cannot legitimately conclude that his wife is an "experienced" woman because the hymen is no longer intact.

The case for remaining silent would rest partially on this fact. In addition, the young lady need not incriminate herself and reveal past sins. Then, too, revelation of her past might cause him to become upset, to reject her, or, later on in marriage, to hold this against her in a moment of anger. This naturally presumes there is little possibility of his knowing from other sources about her indiscretion.

A modern expert on marriage counsels in the opposite vein. He feels that absolute sincerity and openness between the engaged boy and girl are fundamental. They need to accept each other as they are. This means forgiving one another totally, and understanding past mistakes. The danger of discovery, he feels, from some other source also is present. The woman, furthermore, may drive this deep within her, continue to fear he eventually will find out, and then completely lose confidence in her honesty and truthfulness with him.

The predicament described is a perfect example of the impossibility in giving unwavering, black-and-white solutions to certain of life's problems. Only the individual girl is in a position to evaluate the multiple conditions present and judge the best solution available. The counselor's task is to point out aspects she may have been unaware of, aid her in estimating different factors, and confirm her in the final decision.

The young man with a checkered past must face the same question. It may not strike him as intensely as it does the young woman. But it is there.

Let God Forgive You

Which is more important, to forgive yourself or to let God forgive you? It would make an interesting debate. More importantly, however, both kinds of forgiveness are necessary for personal peace and emotional growth. At least the God-believing individual needs his Lord's mercy and acceptance as well as his own self-forgiveness.

The story of God's relations with mankind as recorded in the Bible constantly reads something like this: God loves man first. He demonstrates his love in some visible manner—by creating man, protecting him, giving him special gifts—manna from heaven, the promised land, deliverance from sickness or disease. The Lord seeks in return man's love. Man's loving response to God's love is to be proven through observance of commandments or other directives given from on high. Man more or less responds. In some cases the failure to return God's love and the rejection or, worse, the spurning and neglect of the Creator's laws are serious. God punishes his creatures, hoping to bring them to their senses. Man repents, God forgives and continues to love rather ungrateful man and to bestow singular blessings upon him. Adam and Eve, Noah, Moses, David—these and many others reflect that pattern of God loving man, man failing to live up to his duties to respond with love, and God forgiving man and loving him again.

The account of David and his love for Bathsheba (2 Sam. 11-12 or 2 Kgs. 11-12) is a classic example. King David, selected and anointed by God as the leader of the Chosen People, sent Joab and his servants out to battle as he remained in Jerusalem. "It happened, late one afternoon, when David arose from his couch and was walking upon the roof of the king's house, that he saw from the roof a woman bathing; and the woman was very beautiful. He inquired about this lady, Bathsheba, sent for her, made love to her. She returned home and later sent word to David, 'I am with child.' "

David summoned Uriah her husband from the battlefront. He hoped he would sleep with his wife and thus remove suspicion from the king as the child's father. But the noble soldier felt he could not go to his home, eat, drink and lie with his wife while his leader and fellow comrades in arms were camping in an open field. Frustrated, David invited Uriah to his palace, gave him food and drink and "made him drunk." Still the soldier did not go down to his house.

The king then sent Uriah back to the front with a letter for his commander. He instructed him to place Bathsheba's husband in the front lines, where the fighting was hardest, "and then draw back from him, that he may be struck down, and die." The deed was done.

"When the wife of Uriah heard that Uriah her husband was dead, she made lamentation for her husband. And when the mourning was over, David sent and brought her to his house, and she became his wife, and bore him a son. But the thing that David had done displeased the Lord."

God sent Nathan to the sinning king. This prophet told David a parable about two men, one rich, the other poor. The rich man dealt the poor one a severe blow, unjustly taking his only possession, a small lamb. "Then David's anger was greatly kindled against the man; and he said to Nathan, 'As the Lord lives, the man who has done this deserves to die; and he shall restore the lamb fourfold, because he did this thing, and because he had no pity.' "

Apparently David did not see the parallel with his own sin. Nathan drove the point home and said to the king, "You are the man. Thus says the Lord, the God of Israel, 'I anointed you king over Israel, and I delivered you out of the hand of Saul; and I gave you your master's house, and your master's wives into your bosom, and gave you the house of Israel and of Judah; and if this were too little, I would add to you as much more. Why have you despised the word of the Lord, to do what is evil in his sight?' "

Nathan continued God's message to David with predictions of punishments that will come to the king because he had despised the Lord and took Uriah's wife to be his own. The sword will never depart from his house, evil will rise up in his home, neighbors will take David's wives and lie openly with them in the sun. David had committed his sin secretly; in punishment these deeds will be done clearly before all of Israel.

Chastised and repentant, David says to Nathan, "I have sinned against the Lord."

Nathan then speaks of God's forgiveness, but adds that a continuing punishment will afflict David because of his sin. "The Lord has also put away your sin; you shall not die. Nevertheless, because by this deed you have utterly scorned the Lord, the child that is born to you shall die."[11]

Centuries later this same process seems to continue. Men wander away from God, finally return and seek mercy, are freely forgiven. But often there is a residue, a lingering penalty. Not necessarily the death of a child or a constant stream of physical afflictions, but anguish of conscience, occasional qualms about the past. The unwed mother, the unfaithful husband, the indiscreet wife, the experimenting adolescent — these people may have forgiven themselves and accepted God's forgiveness. Yet is it possible to forget totally? Or are there always moments, brief ones, when perhaps an intense or a slightly disturbing feeling makes us twinge inwardly? Can we eliminate those sporadic, misgiving reflections on our past life? Time heals wounds and erases memories, good and bad ones. But do scars now and then appear? Is this, in a modern way, the continuing punishment that David suffered?

The Christian, in his quest for God's forgiveness, can seek additional comfort in the New Testament. The very name of our Lord is Jesus which means savior. The angel said to Joseph that Mary, his wife, was to conceive. ". . . She will bear a son, and you shall call his name Jesus, for he will save his people from their sins" (Matt. 1:20-21).[12]

The Gospel accounts contain multiple examples of Jesus Christ exercising forgiveness. There are something like 17 different instances in which the Savior actually forgave a sinner or mentioned God's mercy. In chapter 15 of St. Luke, his critics remarked, "This man receives sinners and eats with them." The criticism prompted Jesus to preach on God's forgiveness and to illustrate that teaching, according to his custom, with parables. "Just so, I tell you, there will be more joy in heaven over one sinner who repents than over ninety-nine righteous persons who need no repentance."[13] He then fortified his teaching with the famous story of the prodigal son.

The good thief on the cross knew instant and total forgiveness. Impetuous Peter, swearing he would never deny his Lord and almost immediately denying him three times when put to the test, still experienced the Master's mercy. Later, after the Resurrection, chagrined Peter, questioned about his love, responded, "Yes, Lord, you know that I love you." Jesus' response, forgiving him, even granting him a place of eminence, simply commanded, "Feed my lambs, feed my sheep" (John 21:15-17).[14]

The Gospels are so rich with the forgiving words and actions of Jesus Christ that it is difficult to pick and choose, or to know when to stop. In the next chapter we will describe in detail the story of the Lord with Mary Magdalene. This brief analysis should, however, convince the young (or old) Christian that sincere sorrow, repentance, faith will obtain from God quick and lasting forgiveness.

I never did mention what finally happened between Tony Wood and Ann Phillips on that summer Saturday evening in the car. But suppose, in a calmer moment, they had agreed that waiting for marriage was the best thing for them. Suppose they had decided even further that in their "making-out" they would keep matters under pretty strict control. Suppose they both came to these conclusions and then, on that evening, in the moonlight, next to the lake, they just gave in. Suppose Ann, against her better judgment, flung herself back into Tony's arms. Suppose Tony allowed that emotional tidal wave to drown out his flickering voice of conscience and let himself go completely. What then? What comes later? Guilty feelings, a sense of failure?

This chapter has looked at just that possibility. Ann and Tony, I presumed, established high sexual ideals for themselves, but they also were personally weak and felt the pressures of a modern society which makes it difficult to follow those lofty principles. Their noble goal demands strength and courage. It also requires self-acceptance, learning through mistakes, and (for many or most) confident trust in God's forgiveness.

There remain to cover, in this book, a few practical steps which may help young lovers like Tony and Ann surmount the obstacles to premarital chastity which human weakness, deep mutual feelings, and contemporary civilization place in the way.

9. Charting the Course Ahead

*T*heodore C. Sorensen's huge and highly successful book, *Kennedy*, paints a detailed picture of the late President. Eleven years as advisor, confidant and friend gave the author a gradually increasing understanding of John F. Kennedy's thoughts and feelings. He found the President a vastly complex man, apparently distant and cool to newcomers in the beginning. But Sorensen discovered as time went on that "the more one knew Jack Kennedy, the more one liked him."[1]

The course of history has now made him a hero, martyr, even a saint for many. He probably is smiling at this premature canonization. His biographer noted, "Nor did he, in his moments of utmost pride and solemnity, ever pretend to be free from human vices and imperfections; and he would not want me to so record him. Like Lincoln's a hundred years earlier, his language and humor could be as coarse in private conversation as they were correct on the public platform. He followed Franklin's advice of 'early to bed, early to rise' only when he could not otherwise arrange his schedule."[2]

Kennedy's cold, calculating actions and reserve gave outsiders an impression that his heart was of stone, that he was a man devoid of sentiment, tenderness or deep feeling. There was strong discipline of his feelings, it is true, but Sorensen remarks, "I also learned in time that this cool, analytical mind was stimulated by a warm, compassionate heart. Beneath the careful pragmatic approach lay increasingly deep convictions on basic goals and unusual determination to achieve them."[3] Some took his refusal to display emotion as lack of concern. This irked Kennedy. He complained of James MacGregor Burns's comments about this seeming absence of feeling or commitment. "Burns seems to feel that unless somebody overstates or shouts to the top of their voice they are not concerned about the matter."[4] The truth of the situation seems to lie more in this assertion: "He disliked emotion, not because he felt lightly but because he felt deeply."[5]

Growth in a man is perhaps the ultimate sign of greatness. Sorensen in his treatment of Kennedy emerging as a man extensively describes his leader-friend's continual growth in all areas of life. The late President saw the need for this sustained progress. "We all learn, from the time you are born to the time you die . . . events change . . . conditions change, and . . . you would be extremely unwise . . . to pursue policies that are unsuccessful."[6] This philosophy of constant development and learning was not limited to politics.

I frankly admit a great admiration for the late President. That esteem possibly makes the following comparison or parallel somewhat forced. But I feel that several elements noted above — the presence of imperfections and human vices in Kennedy, the man's deep sentiments combined with strong discipline of those feelings, his continual growth as a man and his willingness to learn from personal mistakes and from the wisdom of others — carry special meaning for young men and women.

In this chapter, I am still concerned with those young persons, with the human vices and imperfections they know, with their struggle to direct and control, deep, tender feelings. I am talking about that future generation of Americans who, in this specific realm of sexual behavior, wish to develop increasingly deep convictions on basic goals and who need unusual determination in the modern world to achieve them. They need to learn from their own mistakes, as I have mentioned, but they also need to learn from others. This final portion of the book, an extension of the last chapter, offers a few positive and constructive aids for the couple struggling to maintain premarital chastity.

Love Is Walking Hand in Hand

The dust jacket of Myron Brenton's book, *The American Male* (quoted extensively in earlier portions of this book), describes its content a bit further: "A Penetrating Look at the Masculinity Crisis." In a chapter investigating "Potency and Sexual Revolution," the author arrives at some conclusions that our anonymous contributors in Chapter 7 deduced from their own personal experiences.

"Furthermore, the emphasis our culture places on explicit sex obscures the fact that an erotic interchange isn't circumscribed by the dimensions of the bedroom. A look, a touch, walking along the street together, or enjoying a meal together — all such acts can evoke a sensuousness, quite satisfying in itself, in two persons free enough within themselves and aware enough of each other to allow such a basic response. The emphasis on sexual intercourse — the close association between sex and masculinity — often causes the American male to forget that sexuality isn't limited to coitus. When I asked the clinicians to tell what is the chief complaint of wives about their husbands, the common reply was: 'He doesn't look at me as a woman. He doesn't make me feel like a woman.' Needless to say, many such wives complain bitterly about their lack of sex life. But much more than sex is involved when they are sexually ignored. Their main feeling is one of being rejected as women. When the husbands begin to pay more attention and overtly acknowledge their wives as desirable females, the women themselves often become much less concerned about actually engaging in sexual intercourse. They no longer cast doubts on their husbands' potency or keep badgering them to exhibit it."[7]

Brenton's observations suggest a helpful and healthy channel for couples in love to divert their feelings. They also emphasize the enormously difficult task before them. As one young woman about to marry remarked, "As feelings grew between us, there also came a great feeling of closeness — I think, when you care for someone, it's natural to want to 'let them know' by physical impulse." As the engagement or courtship moves on, familiarity with each other increases and the desire to express one's inner feelings by physical actions becomes more and more intense. This is, obviously, the way it should be. It would be quite unreasonable to assume that couples on the day before their wedding will lack any desire for the physical and 24 hours later will suddenly find this urge mushrooming into full bloom. This fundamental and natural impulse to express physically, sexually, one's love is further increased by the multiplicity of cultural factors which I have discussed in preceding chapters.

We have said often enough that love and sex are not identical. Sex is meant to be an expression of love. A beautiful and unique expression, too, but not the sole manifestation of a self-giving love. Learning to sublimate feelings and to express them in a variety of ways beyond petting and actual intercourse can help relieve the tension a couple senses. A look, a touch, a meal together, talking on the telephone, doing something he likes to do which she doesn't particularly enjoy, sharing what she enjoys even though he does not care for it, preparing a meal for him, baking him a cake, knitting him a sweater, sending her a card, bringing her a small present, simply noting how pretty she looks — the list is limitless, limited only by the ingenuity of the lover.

There is a further advantage in this sublimation of physical feelings. Later, in married life, couples will be called on to restrain themselves for a variety of reasons. The menstrual period, weeks immediately before and after childbirth, ill health, old age can mean an abstinence from intercourse for a short or long space of time. The couple who have trained themselves before marriage to see in many little actions rich expressions of their love should find these moments of enforced reserve less painful and frustrating. *Life*'s story of Margareta and Willy Falk, quoted earlier, illustrates our point. "It is very hard to be much of a couple toward the end of a pregnancy, and all I could think of was that we would be ourselves again." So her husband commented in the hospital waiting room.

Communion

This section and the next one on confession will probably hold limited interest for the reader who is not a Roman Catholic. They presuppose some understanding of Catholic teaching on the Holy Eucharist and on the sacrament of Penance. The final portion of the chapter, "Address Unknown," should, however, carry universal appeal.

I do not know any teacher or guide foolish enough to attempt a definition of married love. One fares better by simply describing elements necessary for marital happiness or sketching what love in marriage really means. Communication more and more comes to the surface today as *the* indispensable element. It is an obvious fact of experience that love tends to union. Couples in love are happy when together and sad when separated. However, that union of togetherness may be on many levels — physical, emotional, intellectual, spiritual. Communicating with each other means a mutual sharing in any of these areas — a sharing of pleasures and feelings, of ideas, of hopes and disappointments. Whatever strengthens the lines of communication will normally solidify the bonds of matrimony.

Mutual prayer stands high on the list. The couple who pray together may find this further unites them. Prayer, in essence, means communication with God and joint prayer means a sort of intercommunication between God and the two lovers. It is rather difficult to retire in anger when husband and wife pray in union at the end of a day. Beginning the practice before marriage can establish healthy patterns that may continue long after the nuptial service.

For a Roman Catholic the summit of prayer or worship is participating in the celebration of the Holy Eucharist. Often two young lovers quite naturally drift into the habit of going together to Sunday Mass. That phenomenon occurs even when previous church attendance had been sporadic. There is much to commend this. It tends to place the whole courtship in a sacred and serious context. It encourages them to pray together and to talk and think with concern about marriage and its responsibilities. It can also, obviously, reestablish standards of premarital conduct that may have been forgotten or ignored, and supply the couple with spiritual strength to follow those renewed ideals.

Full sharing in Mass presumes receiving the Lord's body and blood in Holy Communion. This serves further to unite the man and woman in love. Sound theological reasons support such an assertion. In John 6, Jesus talked to his followers and to others about the Eucharist.

> "I am the bread of life. Your fathers ate the manna in the wilderness, and they died. This is the bread which comes down from heaven, that a man may eat of it and not die. I am the living bread which came down from heaven; if any one eats of this bread, he will live forever; and the bread which I shall give for the life of the world is my flesh. . .
>
> ". . . He who eats of my flesh and drinks my blood has eternal life, and I will raise him up at the last day. For my flesh is food indeed, and my blood is drink indeed. He who eats my flesh and drinks my blood abides in me, and I in him."[8]

Holy Communion, then, as Christ clearly mentions, brings us into intimate union with him. It is but a step beyond to recognize that those who communicate are, by that very action, brought into close union with one another. St. Paul in 1 Corinthians 10:16-17 emphasizes this truth.

> "The cup of blessing which we bless, is it not a participation in the blood of Christ? The bread which we break, is it not a participation in the body of Christ? Because there is one bread, we who are many are one body, for we all partake of the one bread."[9]

The lesson should not be lost on young lovers. Praying side by side at Mass Sunday after Sunday, and partaking together regularly of the Lord's body and blood bring both of them into a close, personal relationship with God, with Christ. This union with the same Jesus in Communion likewise gives an additional way in which they feel and are, in fact, united with each other.

From a purely pragmatic point of view, couples sometimes find the practice of regular Mass and Communion together offers added motivation for chaste behavior on dates the night or nights beforehand. They strive a bit harder to keep matters under control and thus avoid the necessity of "having" to go to confession before Sunday.

In stressing and encouraging Holy Communion as a helpful means in maintaining premarital chastity, we need to avoid the connected danger of treating the Eucharist with a kind of magical superstition. It is, occasionally at least, suggested that Communion will conquer sins of impurity, that receiving the Eucharist works miracles in the physical, sexual realm. The Church Fathers, whose ancient writings so near to early Christian times deserve special consideration, apparently indicate this. They often speak of the Lord's body and blood as a protection against the onslaughts of the flesh and the temptations of concupiscence. However, very probably such statements simply mean that Holy Communion produces in the heart of man an increase of love both for God and for his fellowman. Such growth in love consequently tends to strengthen a person's ability to control the natural stirrings of the body.

Moreover, to grow in love for God and for one's fellowman means to possess a more open heart, an increased social awareness, a fuller self-giving, self-donating spirit, a better understanding of our neighbor as a person. Such developments denote, actually, progress in the direction of personal maturity. The truly mature man finds his maturity extending in all directions and embracing every area of life. He with relative ease and certainty controls and directs his life and activities. That kind of maturity likewise enables him now better to control and to direct his sexual drives and feelings.

Frequent reception of the Eucharist, therefore, draws a young couple more closely to their God and to each other. It also intensifies the union between the couple and God, expands their hearts, deepens their maturity and, as a consequence, smooths and softens the struggle for premarital chastity.

Confession

Leslie Rawlings' once-only sexual experience with the boy from Harvard produced deep guilt feelings. "I grew so disgusted with myself afterwards, and so sorry

that I had let my curiosity get the better of me." She
was bothered, but bottled the troubled sentiments within. Yet there was a crying desire to unburden her
heart. "I've wanted to tell somebody about that ever
since it happened." Apparently she either had no confidant to whom she could confess her lapse or no courage to reveal her regretted experiment in sex. "Yes,
don't you see, I haven't been able to tell anybody. . ."

Rabbi Michael Kind supplied both the courage and
the confidant. Leslie trusted him.

> ". . . But this is so safe. This is practically
> made to order. You're a rabbi and I'm a . . . a
> *shickseh,* and we'll probably never see each other
> again. It's even better than if I were a Catholic
> telling it to a priest hidden behind a screen in a
> confessional because I *know* the kind of person
> you are."[10]

We mentioned in the last chapter the importance of
self-forgiveness for both progress and peace in sexual
matters. Unburdening a past lapse to someone seems
to make a sinner feel much better and facilitates this
honest forgiveness of one's self. Certainly the theory
and practice of modern psychiatry verify this beyond
doubt. Many of the trained psychiatrist's or counselor's hours are spent in listening. A book basically
for priests on *Counselling the Catholic* devotes an entire chapter to "The Priest as a Listener." Some of
this listening is done in the rectory office; much is done
in the confessional box.

Those who approach the Roman Catholic Church
out of mere curiosity or earnest desire have, in the
past, labeled confession, the sacrament of Penance, one
of the great obstacles to acceptance of Catholicism. The
evident difficulty of revealing embarrassing transgres-
sions to another human being remains. The secrecy of
the confessional seal helps. And the fact that the priest
is simply a man acting in the place of God and his
authority makes it more understandable. Still, no one,
including this priest, likes to admit and reveal inner
weaknesses and humiliating failures. But acceptance
of the theory of confession comes easier today. The
valuable therapy in talking to another about problems

has been experienced, perhaps in very small matters with a high school friend or in serious affairs with a business associate. Revelation of deeper guilt feelings and anxieties about matters affecting one's relationship with God as a step farther does not seem terribly unreasonable.

The confessional, obviously, does give the Roman Catholic an opportunity to reveal personal, sinful failures to this man, to this priest who, in his or her eyes, represents God and takes his place. The priest-confessor who simply listens sympathetically in administering the sacrament has already done much for the troubled penitent. The priest-confessor who understands and wisely assists the anxious person in confession does even more.

Valuable in itself simply as an occasion to express deeply hidden guilt feelings to another, the sacrament of Penance, for the believing Roman Catholic, offers still more permanent and definite aid. The honestly sorry and sincerely converted sinner receives absolution from the Lord through the lips and arm of the priest. He kneels in the confessional, relates his sins, listens to the counsel of the confessor, accepts the penance assigned and listens to these words:

> "May our Lord Jesus Christ absolve you and
> I absolve you from every bond to the extent of
> my power and your need. Finally, I absolve you
> from your sins in the name of the Father, and of
> the Son, and of the Holy Spirit."

The priest raises his right arm as he recites this formula of absolution and makes the Sign of the Cross toward the kneeling penitent as he does so. Ideally (participation of the laity in the liturgical rites such as confession have not everywhere progressed to this ideal state), the penitent responds with an "Amen" indicating his belief in this rite, his sorrow, his desire to receive forgiveness from God.

The priest continues with a prayer for the forgiven sinner.

> "May the Passion of our Lord Jesus Christ,
> the merits of the Blessed Virgin, and of all the

saints, and whatever good you have done and evil you have endured, be cause for the remission of your sins, the increase of grace, and the reward of life everlasting."

Again, ideally, the penitent should reply with an "Amen."

To take this abstract treatment of the sacrament of Penance and place it in a personal context, I must say that in a dozen priestly years duties as a confessor must stand high on the list of most fulfilling tasks. It is not pious talk or pragmatic propaganda to remark that acutely troubled sinners walk out of the confessional with great relief, a sense of joy and peace, confidence in the total forgiveness of their offenses, renewed determination to live the life their consciences direct. I have seen and heard the exhilarating effect one good confession can have upon a guilt-ridden individual. The anonymous letter which concludes this chapter rather eloquently, I think, exposes the anxious conscience of a young woman and the release and guidance she found in the sacrament of Penance.

But it takes courage and a proper view of the confessional.

The proper notion of this sacrament must connect Jesus Christ with the priest who hears, with the priest who absolves. It is, therefore, absolutely essential to keep a clear picture of our Lord as merciful, forgiving Savior before one's eyes. Few Gospel stories do this as well as the familiar incident of Mary Magdalene (Luke 7:36-50).[11]

We are not really sure her name was Mary Magdalene. On July 22 the Roman liturgy of the Catholic Church does celebrate a feast of St. Mary Magdalene, Penitent, the sister of Lazarus who was raised by Christ to life after he had been dead for four days. But considerations make her identification less certain. It does not matter. The incident is one of love and forgiveness and that does matter.

A religious leader of the time named Simon invited Jesus to dinner at his home somewhere in Galilee. The reason for the invitation is not immediately evident. Mere curiosity about this man who was going about doing good and teaching strange doctrines may have prompted Simon; hostility, an attempt to trap Christ in some false move or doctrine, likewise may have been a motive. Trusting admiration did not seem to enter into the picture. He failed to extend to Jesus the courtesies a man of the East customarily offered a distinguished guest. In the case of a prominent person, his feet would be washed upon entrance into the home, he would be embraced and kissed by the master of the house, and his head would be sprinkled with perfume before he sat down at the table. Simon offered none of these to Jesus.

To understand the incident adequately we need to familiarize ourselves with the customs of dining then current. Dinner was served in a room with a U-shaped table in the middle. Guests reclined on small sofas with legs stretched away from the table. Servants passed the food from the opposite side as those present rested on one arm and ate with the other. Banquets were also semipublic affairs in which interested persons were free to enter, observe the proceedings, admire the food, and listen to the conversation. Mary was one of them.

What was she like? "A woman of the city, who was a sinner." A sinner? What kind of one?

That's all the Bible says of her. Merely a woman who did not carefully observe the strict religious precepts expected then? They were called sinners. A prostitute, a harlot, a woman of the streets? Not very likely. That kind of a woman would not have been allowed into the house at all. An immoral woman, one of doubtful reputation? Vague, but that is probably the best bet. In any event, she was a sinner.

Mary came to the banquet prepared. She brought an "alabaster flask of ointment." Apparently the message of Jesus and the kindness of the man were well known to her. She knew the strictness of his words and that urgent summons to an inner conversation of heart, which formed the theme of his preaching. But his tender warmth and understanding, his ready forgiveness of unfortunate sinners also were now famous attributes. Mary had some hope in her misery. Simon's home and banquet gave her the occasion to express honest repentance in a very feminine fashion.

". . . And standing behind him at his feet, weeping, she began to wet his feet with her tears, and wiped them with the hair of her head, and kissed his feet, and anointed them with the ointment."

Her actions upset, or at least puzzled, Simon. He said to himself, "If this man were a prophet, he would have known who and what sort of woman this is who is touching him, for she is a sinner."

Jesus noted the concern on his host's face and said: "Simon, I have something to say to you."

Simon, somewhat startled, responded, "What is it, Teacher?"

"A certain creditor had two debtors; one owed five hundred denarii, and the other fifty. When they could not pay, he forgave them both. Now which of them will love him more?"

The answer was obvious. "The one to whom he forgave more."

"You have judged rightly. . . Do you see this woman? I entered your house, you gave me no water for my feet, but she has wet my feet with her tears and wiped them with her hair. You gave me no kiss, but from the time I came in she has not ceased to kiss my feet. You did not anoint my head with oil, but she has anointed my feet with ointment. Therefore, I tell you, her sins, which are many, are forgiven, for she loved much; but he who forgives little, loves little."

The example coupled with Jesus' commentary was a stinging rebuke to the righteous, but unloving Simon. That aspect of the story does not concern us here. Christ's compassionate treatment of the sinful woman does.

He turned to her, awkward, chagrined as the center of attention, and briefly, but authoritatively, stated, "Your sins are forgiven."

The assembled guests murmured among themselves over this unheard-of action. "Who is this, who even forgives sins?"

But Jesus continued, applying further forgiving oil upon the sinful but repentant woman's heart and feelings. "Your faith has saved you; go in peace."

* * * *

In the construction of new churches and confessional boxes, it would be wise to brighten their usually dismal appearance. Some image of Christ as the forgiving Lord — with the woman taken in adultery, or the prodigal son, or Mary Magdalene — suitably positioned over the entrance to the priest's portion of the confessional or over the entire area, could help fix in penitents' minds the notion that the sacrament of Penance is meant to be, essentially, a joyful experience. It is a homecoming, the embrace of a parent welcoming the wandering child back into the fold, our acceptance by a loving Father and forgiving Savior. It is, in fact, meeting Jesus who says through the lips of the priest, "Your sins are forgiven. Your faith has saved you; go in peace."

The errant man or woman who identifies with Mary Magdalene, in her sins ("which are many") and more in her conversion ("for she loved much"), and who sees the same Christ in the person of the priest-confessor, should find confession no longer a source of anxiety or fear, but a means of peace and support in the turbulent days of courtship.

* * * *

Even with this correct and consoling view of the confessional, however, some obstacles stand in the way. The young boy or girl, man or woman, may have developed a few ideas, partially true but mainly false, which deter him or her from seeking help in the confessional during the search for sexual peace and maturity.

1. *"There's no point in being a hypocrite. What's the use of going to confession when I know I am going right out and do it again?"*

That reaction represents probably the most common sentiment which prevents a troubled person from approaching the sacrament of Penance. The truth present in the statement, important and praiseworthy, abhors phoniness, the absence of an honest effort to improve and correct a mistake. The prospect of being a hypocritical Catholic, running in to confession and out to immediate failure, is disconcerting to say the least. The person caught in some strong situation (engagement, first love that has run out of control, involvement with a partner already married) feels it is better to make the break totally and entirely on one's own before going to God and seeking forgiveness. The honesty here is truly commendable.

God wants us to do our part, of course, but he is quite willing to do more than his share. The troubled individual in this case is not letting God and the confessional do enough. She, for example, may think like this: "I am quite sure that sometime next week, or next month, given the right situation of time and place and mood, I will simply be unable to stand seeing my boyfriend or fiancé upset, frustrated, suffering. I will want to please him. I will want to, for the time at least, relieve his frustration. So I feel quite sure I will slip again. So this means I am not really sorry, nor do I really intend to improve."

Being repentant now and knowing or at least inwardly predicting to myself that I will stumble again are not contradictory. The only requirement for a true and sincere confession is the here and now regret for past errors and a sincere desire to overcome those failings. Practical measures, naturally, need to be taken to avoid pitfalls, but the whole notion of human weakness we have described earlier should make it absolutely evident that the best of men do not always keep their resolutions. That hardly makes the good resolve false and hypocritical.

Michael Kind bitterly and sincerely resolved not to have sex again until he fell in love. Five months later, on a country road off the Wilbur Cross Parkway, he broke his vow. Was Michael a phony, a hypocrite, when he made that promise? I think not. Was he a phony, a hypocrite, when he broke that promise? I think not. Weak, immature, confused, egged on by modern society and its pressures—perhaps one of these. But not phony and hypocritical.

The Catholic who crawls back to confession time after time should not be called phony or hypocritical either. Courageous and well-intentioned would be my words for it.

2. *"I tried for a while. But then we fell again one night and after that it was so easy, we sort of stopped trying."*

Confession should not be seen simply as a cleansing from past sins. It means total conversion of the whole person. The sacrament does bring peace, naturally, but it also can and should offer strength and renewed determination for the challenge ahead. The struggling couple, far from making a mockery of confession, are, instead, allowing God and this sacrament to help them. Returning swiftly after a lapse, they thus are restored with equal swiftness to peace of soul. The short but positive encouragement of an understanding confessor may further deepen their motivation in moments of weakness. The grace of God, communicated through this visible sign of mercy and forgiveness, can strengthen their love for God and for each other and supply additional courage when powerful factors tend to pull them away from standards they have set for themselves.

Experience verifies that the person who has fallen, who feels upset and guilty or troubled, psychologically is a sitting duck for the next temptation which comes along.

The individual who confesses frequently may very well continue to fail; but quite likely will fail less often.

3. *"I was so confused. It seemed so beautiful. Why can anything be wrong that is so wonderful?"*

The reaction, particularly of a girl, to the initial sexual experience surrounded by love many times causes a certain crisis of faith. I have, earlier, described this phenomenon. Suddenly all that may have been seen as ugly and bad becomes beautiful and good: therefore, how can it be wrong? Perhaps the Church is wrong. I must be losing my faith. There is no point in going to confession, even to Mass in my state.

Reassurance is needed. After all, kissing, petting, intercourse can be magnificent means of physical, psychological, emotional union and tenderness. The wedding ceremony does not supply some added miraculous element to transform an action that on Friday was cold and unattractive into an identical activity that on

Saturday night in the wedding bed becomes warm and compelling. The couple who have stumbled along this line look back upon their evening as a rich and wonderful experience. Deep down they do not see how they can be sorry and regret something that was so profoundly moving and fulfilling. Must they feel bad and sad about the goodness of their action? Does true sorrow, the requisite for sacramental absolution, demand an utter detestation of their action, a sense that they have committed some terrible deed? Psychologically speaking, that would be difficult, if not impossible, for the two lovers.

Or is it sufficient that they simply regret the wrongness of the action, the fact that it was done out of the security and permanent promise of marriage, that it was a true, deep love whose expression on an occasion temporarily ran out of control? Does not the mere fact that the individual is here in confession, sincerely determined to keep these displays of affection better directed in the days ahead, prove sorrow for the past lapse from established goals? I think so.

I believe couples in love are tremendously reassured when told that what they have done was beautiful, even though wrong. Such advice also prepares them realistically for the increasing struggle to control feelings as their courtship and engagement progress. They then can understand that the sometimes almost overwhelming impulse sweeping upon them is but the pattern expected in a developing love between man and woman. Recognizing the manner in which the desire to express inner sentiments grows, the couple may also realize the imaginative and practical efforts needed to sublimate and channel this desire for the time being. It can be rough going, to say the least. As we said earlier, courage is pretty essential at this point.

4. *"I was so ashamed, I just could not get up the courage to come to confession. It took me a long time before I could come here."*

This quizzical response to the question, "Why did you put off confession for so long?" is not uncommon. Many times the presence of this deep shame, guilt, embarrassment—call it what you will—is all that apparently restrains the troubled Catholic from reaching for the sacrament where peace and freedom can be discovered. The wrongful liaison may long have been severed, the legitimate, but out-of-control courtship broken, the overinvolved sexual activity now brought into acceptable patterns—and still the person holds back.

Invariably the individual also knows that calm and forgiveness can, in his instance, only be successfully found in confession. Yet there is a delay or a wait. Frequently some discussion with a close friend about the problem supplies the initial push. He encourages the tormented person to go to confession and get it off his mind. He may recommend some specific priest who enjoys the reputation as an understanding confessor. He offers to go along on a Saturday afternoon or evening for moral support. Finally the suffering soul summons courage, nervously makes the trip to church, stands anxiously in line, then with hesitation and perhaps a few tears, pours out the sin or sins. Suddenly, the guilt feelings all seem so far away; the lengthy delay so foolish and unnecessary. Months of anguish could have been avoided. But at least now there is a weight lifted, a burden removed.

I really know of no simple solution to help the sinner seeking confessional absolution but afraid or ashamed to make the move. A sermon now and then stressing the merciful nature of Christ and confession, lines like this in a book, religion classes emphasizing the true and positive picture of this sacrament, sympathy, kindness and understanding as a confessor—these may pave the way. But ultimately, I suppose, the individual must face the facts himself and courageously make the move.

5. *"It was the first time this ever happened. I didn't know how to confess that kind of a sin and was embarrassed."*

Some of this stems from our past, faulty sex instructions. The situation has vastly improved over the past decade or two. Sensible, positive classes spread over the 12 years and even on to college, suitably adapted to the level of the listener, are increasingly the practice. Records, movies, books, pamphlets are easily available.

But there still is a bit of a problem.

The teacher, priest, parent hesitates to describe *all* the sexual aberrations possible. It is one thing to present a positive picture of how sex fits into the overall plan of love and life. It is quite another to detail, at length, various departures from the plan. However, today's openness in the press, television and theater leaves little to the imagination of the adolescent. The earlier philosophy avoided mention of things like masturbation or homosexuality with the hope that innocent ears would thus not discover previously unheard or unthought of actions. There seems little danger of that in present society. However, the former practice, done in the best of motives, left many individuals confused and awkward. Having done something wrong, the youngster still did not know how to express his sin in confession. He quite naturally then either deferred confession or, worse yet, concealed in his heart the fault probably troubling him the most. The Catholic young man or woman, now troubled by a so-called "bad confession," is in an even more anxious state. The anxieties have been driven deeper. Unraveling that situation takes a little while longer, a bit more courage.

The penitent does not relish describing the details of some sexual lapse, nor does the priest enjoy hearing them. Specifics are not needed for the sacrament, but the penitent, unaware of how to confess his sin, may feel such descriptions are important. That further adds to the embarrassment and hesitation.

To eliminate this obstacle, we give here some brief, simple statements which adequately, for us at least, present the sin committed. If the reader, not a Catholic, finds all this terribly mechanical and legalistic, we are not surprised. Please bear with me. But a concise statement of some general sexual mistakes may help a young reader reach the peace and forgiveness of the sacrament. That, of course, is its purpose. The relation of sins is but a step toward achievement of that goal, and not always an essential one at that (e.g., speechless victim of an accident, soldiers before battle).

"Father, I committed a sin of sex alone on (number) occasions."

"Father, I committed a sin of sex with another

person of the same sex on (number) occasions."

"Father, I committed a sin of sex with a person of the opposite sex. There was excessive necking on (number) occasions. There was light petting on (number) occasions. There was heavy petting on (number) occasions. I had sexual intercourse on (number) occasions."

Light petting includes touches of the breast and genital areas. Heavy petting generally means similar touches but with much more intense activity often resulting in orgasm for the man or woman. A person involved in intercourse need not mention the necking and petting preceding it. The confessor presumes that as a natural part of the total action.

This does not exhaust all possibilities. But it does cover the main ones and should enable one to confess with sufficient information and yet avoid superfluous details that simply serve as a burden to the penitent and to the priest. It is a tragedy that guilt-ridden individuals are deterred from God's mercy freely given in the confessional because of undue attention to these mechanics. Perhaps the above treatment will help avoid that severe, although generally temporary disaster.

6. *"The last time I went to confession, the priest shouted at me. He scolded me and made me feel so bad and so embarrassed. It was such a terrible experience, I have stayed away this long, afraid to go back."*

The priest in confession is *supposed* to deal with the sinner as Christ treated the woman taken in adultery; unfortunately, he may not always in fact act in that manner. Priests, too, are human and unique individuals. Some by nature are more stern than others. Some stress God's holiness and justice and the evil of sin. Others emphasize God's mercy and forgiveness and the beauty of conversion. The same priest moreover experiences variable moods which may affect his handling of confessions on a particular occasion. God does forgive in a divine way through confession. But he also employs flesh-and-blood men as his instruments.

The pain caused by such harsh treatment surely is regrettable. A kind and understanding priest can partially repair the harm and hurt. The only advice to be offered here is to try again. Find another confessor. Probably the maximum freedom in the Catholic Church pertains to a person's selection of a confessor. The penitent being severely chastised, rightly or wrongly, by a priest-confessor may always leave and seek another who may grasp the situation in a different way. The courageous individual might stop a storming priest with a humble whisper, "Father, I feel like Mary Magdalene, I thought you would be like Christ." It seems, however, that these traumatic experiences are more exceptions than the rule. Ample sympathetic priests willing to help a sincerely sorry person are available. The troubled individual will not need to search long or far for relief from the burden weighing down his heart.

In the preceding chapter, we discussed the notion of self-acceptance and forgiveness and its connection with past mistakes. All of this applies with special meaning to the Roman Catholic and confession. Many of the objections and hesitations sketched above arise fundamentally from a lack of self-forgiveness and an unwillingness to let God forgive. Rehashing past errors, punishing oneself, undergoing all kinds of inner torment often is a cover for self-pity rather than sincere grief for wrong done to one's fellowman. Our tearful remorse may be more a result of injured pride than of our grief at having failed God.

In any event, we need, as Roman Catholics, realistically to admit our mistake, honestly to regret it, courageously to confess it, and confidently to accept God's forgiveness. Then we need to move on.

Address Unknown

There is joy in helping others. The priest can experience that joy; he can help and love in many ways. Sometimes those served and loved are known to him; but many times those helped are nameless people, faceless individuals speaking and listening in the secrecy of the confessional.

A letter from one of these came to the author while he was writing this book. There was no return address. It rather eloquently, I think, endorses through personal experience many points made in this chapter and throughout the book. It offers a final message of wisdom, courage and hope to the generation of young Americans reading these lines.

Dear Father Champlin,

Contained within you will find a summary of a great trial which has occurred in this past year of my life.

I heartily admit a rather grave mistake was made, but many times people must learn from mistakes, and I hope that by giving you a resume of my feelings, I can in some way help others prevent the situation I found myself in.

I am in the process of ending a ten-month engagement, and am about to start a new life as a Mrs. . .

Even before the formal engagement we had trouble. I don't really know how or when it all started.

We had dated for close to two years, and I guess we both knew that we were right for each other.

As feelings grew between us, there also came a great feeling of closeness—it's natural to want to "let them know" by physical means, but there are limits which must not be exceeded outside of marriage.

First, we began to keep late hours, and along with this came sieges of necking and petting.

The next thing I knew I was in the confessional with the problem of extramarital relations.

My feelings were confused—I think my pride was crushed, and the thought of no longer being a "virgin" upset me. I had no one to talk to except my fiancé and you, Father.

I know there were many ways of preventing our situation.

First, I know our engagement was too long. Sex is a beautiful thing and nothing to be abused or tampered with. When two people anticipate marriage, and they just happen to have a taste of sex, it gets harder than ever each time they are together to ignore it.

My biggest advice to all couples is please respect each other—if you start making any type of unacceptable physical passes, it will lead to trouble. The human body is one full of emotions, and each time a "pass" is made, the body wants more. Before you know it, neither person is content until it is too late.

Another piece of advice is to keep active—when you date, go out with others, and try as you can to involve yourself in many activities.

Don't think sex is the most important attribute—you can sublimate your feelings a bit. Do other things for your mate to make him happy, and show him you care.

If you knit, make him a sweater or a pair of red socks, or bake him a cake sometimes. This can bring people close together, too, and by this means, you really get to know each other better.

After our relationship, a great feeling of guilt and shame came over me. No one will ever know how depressed a person can be.

All kinds of notions ran through my head, and the one that bothered me the most was the fear: what if God doesn't bless us with children because of this sin?

Believe me, if it weren't for you, Father, I don't know what I would have done.

My fiancé felt as bad as I did—we are both fairly good Catholics, come from good families, with loving parents, are both of good intellect, and there we were—believe me, it can happen to anyone.

Another big fear I had was that of becoming pregnant. What an insecure feeling that was! How can you carry, and give birth to, and raise a baby knowing he was conceived in a cheap, selfish manner? I just feel the baby would show signs of insecurity somewhere in his life, along with his parents.

And our families, they love us so dearly—what a deep unspoken hurt we could have caused them!

Well, Father, I feel this about summarizes my story. I admit I had to learn the hard way, but at least I learned.

If anyone should ever find themselves nearing this predicament, my advice would be to find a priest-friend as I did.

Don't try to live with feelings within yourself—the relief that God does forgive is the greatest blessing in the world.

Sincerely,
A Penitent

Epilogue

Playwright Robert Anderson has written several plays which touch on sex, love and marriage. In his latest one, *You Know I Can't Hear You When the Water's Running,* he has Chuck remark, "Sex is beautiful . . . one of the greatest blessings of mankind."[1]

Unfortunately, not all Americans speak as glowingly of sex. Myron Brenton, in his book *The American Male,* thinks that part of the reason for our unhealthy attitudes about this subject is the "Sex Bombardment." In the following excerpt, he describes the phenomenon, notes a few of its deleterious effects, and suggests a possible remedy:

"The ceaseless emphasis on and the commercialization of sex—via the mass media, songs, dances, advertising, and even the social sciences—are a powerful force in intensifying the competitive aspects of sex and are destructive in other ways as well. This sex-obsession feature of contemporary American culture is frequently attacked on humanistic and moralistic grounds—i.e., it leads to sexual depersonalization and has unpleasantly voyeuristic connotations. Actually, the obsession with matters sexual is a perfectly understandable phenomenon. Since one extreme reaction usually invites another, the Victorian denial of sex and the current compulsive affirmation of it are simply two sides of the same well-worn coin. If any proof is needed that the American psyche is still imbued with a heavy dose of fear and guilt about sex, this compulsive need to affirm it—to show ourselves 'liberated'—is sufficient evidence. Contemporary America is no more sexually liberated than the Don Juan who has to sleep with every woman crossing his path or the self-styled pornography policeman who sees hard-core smut wherever he turns. Parenthetically, but not insignificantly, despite all the so-called sexual freedom, there's still no realistic, comprehensive sex-education program for young people in the nation's schools."[2]

I have tried, in this book, to offer some of the positively oriented and psychologically sound sexual education for young people which Brenton sees as so essential. I hope that individuals like Tony Wood and Ann Phillips will find in it some answers or at least the beginning of answers to questions that perplex them. Questions like: "What is love? How do you know you are in love? How do you stay in love? How do you keep that love and make it grow deeper and stronger as the years go on? How do you best express it, before marriage, and afterward? What do you do about mistakes?" Young people ask these questions. And, unfortunately, they do not always receive solutions from their parents.

For example, in an anonymous survey of one of my high school classes one year I learned that 13 out of 30 had received no education or training about sex from their parents and only nine out of the 30 felt the presentation they had been given was adequate. One girl volunteered the information that her education in sex came from a boyfriend and "he used a medical book which his parents gave him." I believe the results of this nonprofessional survey are typical.

At the same time, desirable school-centered sex education, now mushrooming in the United States, should not be considered a panacea for all our sexual ills. *Time* magazine, with a lengthy essay "On Teaching Children About Sex" in its June 9, 1967, issue, had this to say: "There is a growing suspicion that too much may be expected of sex education and that the programs, no matter how sound, are asked to provide solutions to moral problems that are really part of society." Later, speaking to fathers and mothers who are alarmed at the realistic, but seemingly permissive norms for conduct given in sex-education classes, *Time* warns that they should not expect the schools to offer rigid and specific rules. "Parents who feel that these principles are inadequate cannot and should not look to the schools for decisive help. They will have to redefine or reassert their own morality in the home and in society at large."[3]

Perhaps this book will help parents a little with their children and the subject of sex. It is written directly for young adults from late high school years through the middle twenties. But I hope it may indirectly enable parents to understand the thinking of their sons and daughters and to reach them on these sensitive issues. If it could serve as a vehicle to promote open, honest, frank discussion between parent and young son or young daughter, that would be a very fine thing indeed.

The goals or norms of conduct are rather traditional in many ways. I have argued that I felt it is wiser to hold off on sexual intercourse until after marriage. I even went further and suggested, in the words of Father Capon, "something utterly outlandish besides," that it might be beneficial to try to avoid heavy and even light petting until after the nuptial vows.

The most significant purpose of the book, however, is to offer reasons why premarital chastity has value for today's youth. Bishop Fulton J. Sheen, in a memorandum to his priests and people about the training of adolescents, offered two motives for chastity. "Purity should be taught as reverence for the mystery of life and its creativeness, and as respect for personality, so that no person is ever 'used' for pleasure as a torch might be thrown into a city to give the thrill of flames and ashes."[4] My own chapter, "Love and Life," and the entire book, views sex as an expression of love and as something to be used in the service of life.

The book needs to be grasped as a whole unit. I have presented lofty, traditional ideals. Nevertheless, I believe it is more difficult for young people of today to live up to these noble aspirations than it was for their parents or grandparents. The cultural pressures of our sex-obsessed, freedom-rich American society, coupled with age-old human weakness, place an added strain upon them. For that reason, I have given two chapters, the final sections of the book, to this whole question of failures and mistakes. Possibly one of the reasons so many individuals are walking around with excessive guilt feelings and seem preoccupied with the so-called intolerable burden of traditional sexual morality is a lack of stress in our teaching on God's mercy and the importance of self-forgiveness. It seems to me that we should encourage the young to strive for excellence in sexual matters, but that we should at the same time help them to face realistically human failures and personal weakness.

A final word about the frankness of this volume. To those who might object, my only response is this: The audience for whom it is intended demands honesty and frankness above all elements in a writer or a speaker. I base my case on the following testimony.

During the period in which I was writing this book, I used its ideas and quotations in several lectures to students of different backgrounds. One such occasion was in the course of a full day's program on love, sex, courtship, marriage for 500 Catholic high school students. I delivered three talks, conducted a question-and-answer period and supervised a group discussion session. There was an equal mixture of boys and girls from the freshman through the senior years. Several weeks later I received the results of a questionnaire filled out by each one of them giving their opinions on the total program and its various parts. Directions at the top asked them not to sign their names and assured them that only I would read the answers. I want to be pardoned for this bit of self-glorification; the responses should explain why I am quoting them.

One student commented on the frankness: "It was worth the while, even though Father was kind of frank and direct, but now you have to be frank, because most of the teen-agers of today are."

Another seconded this and noted the evasiveness of parents and teachers: "The discussion period satisfied me since life, love and sex were brought into the open. We have been 'segregated' in school concerning these problems and I felt it was about time someone brought facts into the open. Thank you, Father. The whole program, I think, was fabulous. Someone finally had the 'nerve' to bring these questions into the open and to help solve the problems of teen-agers. Everyone else seemed to be evasive on questions concerning sex, but Father really helped many of us out."

A third person evaluated the question-and-answer period: "Great. You answered a lot of questions that I had. Your parents can't really tell you necking, etc., is wrong, they probably aren't sure themselves. And my teachers, well, what a negative attitude!" **This** same individual continued about the overall program: "This is just what we teen-agers need, someone who will be frank. Lots of parents are skittish and your teachers in school just talk around it."

A fourth teen-ager said this: "The lectures were very frank and right to the point. They solved many personal problems for me. There is only one way to express it. It just cleansed my soul, it lifted many doubts from my conscience and relieved my guilt."

This young man both warmed my heart and made me chuckle: "It satisfied me because it showed me that I should not experiment with young ladies as I have in the past. Also—that the girl should not allow me to touch her and should give me a good belt in the mouth if I do. During the group discussion I was with a group of girls and it showed they are not the type to engage in sexual love as some girls might."

The same boy voiced his view on the overall presentation:

"My opinion of the program in general was one of accomplishment and victory over the sin of adultery. I gained an insight into the happenings in the teen-age world today. I also realized the wrong I've done in using my girl as a plaything or something I just have around when I'm 'hot' or sexually aroused. It taught many about the reality of what could and does happen when the necking starts to get a little heavy. Thank you, Father, for showing me what I was doing before it was too late."

A final comment from one of the students:

"I enjoyed the program very much. Father seemed to understand us and didn't look down upon us as a group of 'wild immature babies.' In general it gave you a moral code by which to live. Before I went in there, *sex* to me was a subject *not* to be discussed in public. But Father cleared this up. Sex is nothing to be ashamed of unless it is abused. It is a very beautiful thing sent to us by God."

The defense rests.

Acknowledgments

I would like to thank the following persons and publishers for permission to use copyrighted material from the titles below:

ABINGDON PRESS—*Letters to Karen* by Charlie W. Shedd. Copyright 1965.

ASSOCIATION PRESS—*Why Wait Till Marriage?* by Evelyn Millis Duvall. Copyright 1965 by National Board of Young Men's Christian Association.

CONFRATERNITY OF CHRISTIAN DOCTRINE — Scriptural excerpts from Bible text. Copyright 1952.

DAVID McKAY Co., INC. — *Unmarried Love* by Eustace Chesser. Copyright 1965.

DODD, MEAD & CO.—*Seventeenth Summer* by Maureen Daly. Copyright 1942.

DOUBLEDAY & COMPANY, INC.—Excerpts noted from *The Jerusalem Bible*. Copyright 1966.

FIDES PUBLISHERS, INC.—*Christian Morality Today* by Charles E. Curran. Copyright 1966.

GUILD PRESS, INC.—The excerpt from the Declaration on Christian Education is taken from *The Documents of Vatican II*, published by Guild Press, American Press, Association Press, and Herder and Herder, and copyrighted 1966 by The American Press.

HARPER & ROW, PUBLISHERS, INC.—*The Art of Loving* by Erich Fromm. Copyright 1956.

Profiles in Courage, Memorial Edition, by John F. Kennedy. Copyright 1956 by John F. Kennedy. Copyright 1964 by Robert F. Kennedy.

Kennedy by Theodore Sorensen. Copyright 1965.

HELICON—*The Psychology of Loving* by Ignace Lepp. Copyright 1963.

Life—From "An Empire Built on Sex" by Diana Lurie (October 29, 1965) and from "A Woman on Her Way to a Miracle" by Eleanor Graves (July 22, 1966). Copyright Time, Inc. 1965, 1966.

McCALL CORPORATION — *Redbook* Magazine, July, 1965. Copyright 1965. "How Young Men Influence the Girls Who Love Them" by Mary Calderone.

McINTOSH AND OTIS, INC.—*The Rabbi* by Noah Gordon. Published by McGraw-Hill, Inc. Copyright 1965.

NATIONAL COUNCIL OF THE CHURCHES OF CHRIST — The Scripture quotations so noted in this publication are from the Revised Standard Version of the Bible, Catholic Edition. Copyright 1965 and 1966.

Notes

DEDICATION
1. *Documents of Vatican II.* Walter M. Abbott, S.J., General Editor. New York: The American Press, 1966. Declaration on Christian Education, paragraph 1.

PROLOGUE
1. Susann, Jacqueline. *Valley of the Dolls.* New York: Bantam Books, 1967, p. 23.

CHAPTER 1 LOVE IS A MANY-SPLENDORED THING
1. Gordon, Noah. *The Rabbi.* New York: Fawcett World Library, 1965, p. 379.
2. Lepp, Ignace. *The Psychology of Loving.* Translated by Bernard B. Gilligan. New York: The New American Library, 1963, p. 17.
3. Schulz, Charles M. *Love is Walking Hand in Hand.* San Francisco: Determined Productions, Inc., 1965. Captions for majority of illustrations in the book.
4. Farrow, John. *Damien the Leper.* Garden City, New York: Doubleday and Co., Inc., 1954, p. 122.
5. Fromm, Erich. *The Art of Loving.* New York: Bantam Books, Inc.. 1956, p. 18.
6. *Ibid.,* p. 18.
7. *Ibid.,* p. 19.
8. Revised Standard Version of the Bible, Catholic Edition.
9. *Ibid.*
10. Fromm, *op. cit.,* p. 8.
11. Capote, Truman, *In Cold Blood.* New York: The New American Library, 1965, pp. 323-327.
12. Fromm, *op. cit.,* pp. 23-24.
13. Gordon, *op. cit.,* pp. 78-93.
14. Fromm, *op. cit.,* p. 24.
15. *Ibid.,* p. 24.
16. *The Jerusalem Bible.* Garden City, New York: Doubleday and Co., Inc., 1966, I Corinthians 13.

CHAPTER 2 MEN AND WOMEN ARE DIFFERENT. OR ARE THEY?
1. Lepp, *op. cit.,* p. 143.
2. *Ibid.,* p. 24.
3. Demal, Willibald, O.S.B. *Pastoral Psychology in Practice.* Translated by Joachim Werner Conway. New York: P. J. Kenedy & Sons, 1955, p. 52.
4. Brenton, Myron. *The American Male.* New York: Coward-McCann, 1966, p. 53.
5. *Ibid.,* p. 56.
6. Friedan, Betty. *The Feminine Mystique.* New York: Dell Publishing Co., Inc., 1966, p. 30.
7. *Ibid.,* p. 69.

8. Lepp, *op. cit.*, p. 25.
9. Brenton, *op. cit.*, p. 50.
10. Cavanaugh, John R., M.D. *Fundamental Marriage Counseling.* Milwaukee: Bruce, 1963, p. 92.
11. Brenton, *op. cit.*, pp. 64-65.
12. *Ibid.*, pp. 60-61.
13. Hettlinger, Richard F. *Living With Sex: The Student's Dilemma.* New York: The Seabury Press, 1966, pp. 114-115.
14. Hettlinger, *op. cit.*, pp. 118-119.

CHAPTER 3 PICKING YOUR PARTNER
1. Lepp, *op. cit.*, p. 50.
2. *Ibid.*, p. 52.
3. *Ibid.*, p. 62.
4. *Ibid.*, p. 53.
5. Capote, *op. cit.*, pp. 18-19.
6. Lepp, *op. cit.*, p. 162.
7. Gordon, *op. cit.*, pp. 74-75.

CHAPTER 4 LOVE AND LIFE
1. Peale, Norman Vincent. *Sin, Sex and Self-Control.* Garden City, New York: Doubleday and Co., Inc., 1965, p. 76.
2. Oraison, Marc, M.D. *Learning to Love.* New York: Hawthorn Books, Inc., 1965, pp. 46-47.
3. Gordon, *op. cit.*, pp. 178-179.
4. *Ibid.*, pp. 109-110.
5. Daly, Maureen. *Seventeenth Summer.* New York: Dodd, Mead & Co., 1966, p. 1.
6. Gordon, *op. cit.*, p. 89.
7. *Ibid.*, p. 127.
8. *Ibid.*, pp. 143-144.
9. "An Empire Built on Sex." *Life*, October 29, 1965. With Special Comment by Diana Lurie, p. 70.
10. *Ibid.*, p. 71.
11. Revised Standard Version, Catholic Edition, *op. cit.*
12. *Ibid.*
13. May, Rollo. "Valves in Sexual Love." Excerpts from his forthcoming book, *Love and Will,* to be published by W. W. Norton, appearing in *Marriage*, October, 1965, p. 1 and p. 71.
14. O'Hara, John. *Appointment in Samarra.* New York: The New American Library, 1934, pp. 52-53.
15. Shedd, Charlie W. *Letters to Karen.* Nashville, Tennessee: Abingdon Press, 1965, p. 105.
16. Graves, Eleanor. "A Woman On Her Way To A Miracle." *Life*, July 22, 1966, pp. 48-62B.

CHAPTER 5 WHY WAIT UNTIL MARRIAGE?
1. Milas, Suzanne. "Why I Believe in Sex Before Marriage." *Redbook*, November, 1967, pp. 10-11.
2. Susann, Jacqueline, *op. cit.*, pp. 117-118.

3. "The Pleasures and Pain of Single Life." *Time*, September 15, 1967, p. 27.
4. Chesser, Dr. Eustace. *Unmarried Love.* New York: David McKay Co., 1965, pp. 36-37; 52; 109.
5. Cox, Harvey. *The Secular City.* New York: Macmillan, 1966, pp. 214-215.
6. Confraternity of Christian Doctrine Bible, 1952. Copyright Edition.
7. *Ibid.*
8. Capon, Robert Farrar. *Bed and Board.* New York: Simon and Schuster, 1965, pp. 22-24.
9. Levin, Max, M.D. "The Meaning of Sex and Marriage: A Lecture to College Students." *Current Medical Digest*, August, 1967, pp. 1071-1086.
10. Duvall, Evelyn Millis. *Why Wait Till Marriage?* New York: Association Press, 1965, pp. 32-37.
11. "The Pill." Editorial in Syracuse University *Daily Orange*, September 22, 1966, p. 2.
12. "Negro Illegitimacy Rate Declines." *National Catholic Reporter*, June 21, 1967, p. 6.
13. *A New Catechism.* New York: Herder and Herder, 1967, p. 387.
14. *Ibid.*, p. 388.
15. *Ibid.*, p. 392.
16. Berrigan, Daniel, S.J. *They Call Us Dead Men.* New York: The Macmillan Company, 1966, Chapter 2, "Marriage."
17. Levin, *op. cit.*, pp. 1071-1086.

CHAPTER 6 HOW FAR CAN WE GO?
1. Suenens, Leon Joseph Cardinal. *Love and Control.* Translated by George J. Robinson. Westminster, Maryland: Newman Press, 1963, p. 52.
2. Duvall, *op. cit.*, pp. 29-30.
3. Kavanaugh, James. *A Modern Priest Looks at His Outdated Church.* New York: Trident Press, 1967, pp. 104-113.
4. Hettlinger, *op. cit.*, p. 141.
5. *Ibid.*, p. 148.
6. *Ibid.*, p. 142.
7. Monden, Louis, S.J. *Sin, Liberty and Law.* Translated by Joseph Donceel, S.J. New York: Sheed and Ward, 1965, p. 104.
8. Curran, Charles E. *Christian Morality Today.* Notre Dame, Indiana: Fides Publishers, Inc., 1966, pp. 19-21.
9. deVinck, José. *The Virtue of Sex.* New York: Hawthorn Books, Inc., 1966, pp. 96-97.
10. Calderone, Mary. "How Young Men Influence the Girls Who Love Them." *Redbook* magazine, July, 1965.
11. Hettlinger, *op. cit.*, p. 119.
12. *Ibid.*, p. 124.
13. Kavanaugh, *op. cit.*, p. 111.
14. *Ibid.*, p. 110.
15. Curran, *op. cit.*, p. 20.

16. Hettlinger, *op. cit.*, p. 69.
17. Jone, Heribert, O.F.M. Cap. *Moral Theology*. Translated and adapted by Urban Adelman, O.F.M. Cap. Westminster, Maryland: The Newman Press, 1956, p. 155.

CHAPTER 8 STARTING OVER
1. Revised Standard Version, Catholic Edition, *op. cit.*
2. *Ibid.*
3. Ritual Approved by the National Conference of Bishops of the United States of America. New York: Catholic Book Publishing Co., 1964, p. 379.
4. Gordon, *op. cit.*, pp. 144-145.
5. Kennedy, John F. *Profiles in Courage.* Memorial Edition with a Special Foreword by Robert F. Kennedy. New York: Harper and Row, 1964, p. 1.
6. *Ibid.*, pp. IX-X.
7. *Ingenious Americans.* "Garrett A. Morgan." Number 2 in a series of advertisements sponsored by Old Taylor Distillery Company in *Ebony*, November, 1966, p. 111.
8. Revised Standard Version, *op. cit.*
9. Gordon, *op. cit.*, pp. 179-180.
10. Revised Standard Version, *op. cit.*
11. *Ibid.*
12. *Ibid.*
13. *Ibid.*
14. *Ibid.*

CHAPTER 9 CHARTING THE COURSE AHEAD
1. Sorensen, Theodore C. *Kennedy.* New York: Bantam Books, Inc., 1966, p. 14.
2. *Ibid.*, p. 30.
3. *Ibid.*, p. 13.
4. *Ibid.*, p. 14.
5. *Ibid.*, p. 14.
6. *Ibid.*, p. 27.
7. Brenton, *op. cit.*, pp. 190-191.
8. Revised Standard Version, *op. cit.*
9. *Ibid.*
10. Gordon, *op. cit.*, pp. 179-180.
11. Revised Standard Version, *op. cit.*

EPILOGUE
1. Rubin, Joan Alleman. "Why Does Anybody Stay Married? Playwright Robert Anderson Provides a Thoughtful Answer." *Playbill*, June, 1967, p. 17.
2. Brenton, *op. cit.*, pp. 179-180.
3. "On Teaching Children About Sex." *Time*, June 9, 1967, p. 36.
4. Sheen, Most Rev. Fulton J. Memorandum on Confirmation for the Diocese of Rochester, New York. As published in the *American Journal of Catholic Youth Work*, Spring, 1967, p. 65.

Bibliography

BERTOCCI, PETER A. *Sex, Love & The Person.* New York: Sheed and Ward, 1967.

BRENTON, MYRON. *The American Male.* New York. Coward-McCann, 1966.

CALLAHAN, SIDNEY CORNELIA. *The Illusion of Eve.* New York: Sheed and Ward, 1965.

CAPON, ROBERT FARRAR. *Bed and Board.* New York: Simon and Schuster, 1965.

CAVANAUGH, JOHN R., M.D. *Fundamental Marriage Counseling.* Milwaukee: Bruce, 1963.

COX, HARVEY. *The Secular City.* New York: Macmillan, 1966 (Paperback).

CURRAN, CHARLES E. *Christian Morality Today.* Notre Dame, Ind.: Fides Publishers, Inc., 1966 (Paperback).

DEKRUIJF, T. C. *The Bible On Sexuality.* Translated by F. Vander Heijden. Depere, Wisconsin: St. Norbert Abbey Press, 1966 (Paperback).

DEMAL, WILLIBALD, O.S.B. *Pastoral Psychology in Practice.* Translated by Joachim Werner Conway. New York: P. J. Kenedy & Sons, 1955.

DE VINCK, JOSÉ. *The Virtue of Sex.* New York: Hawthorn Books, Inc., 1966.

DIETZ, FRANCIS X. *What Catholic Girls Should Know About Marriage.* Notre Dame, Indiana: Fides Publishers, Inc., 1960 (Paperback).

DILLON, VALERIE VANCE AND IMBIORSKI, WALTER J. *A Christian Guide to Your Child's Sex Life.* Chicago: Cana Conference of Chicago, 1966 (Paperback).

DUVALL, EVELYN MILLIS. *Why Wait Till Marriage?* New York: Association Press, 1965.

EARNSHAW, GEORGE L. *Serving Each Other in Love.* Valley Forge: The Judson Press, 1967.

FRIEDAN, BETTY. *The Feminine Mystique.* New York: Dell Publishing Co., Inc., 1966 (Dell Paperback). Published originally by W. W. Norton and Co., Inc., New York.

FROMM, ERICH. *The Art of Loving.* New York: Bantam Books, Inc., 1956 (Paperback). Published originally by Harper and Row, Publishers, Inc., New York.

GEISSLER, EUGENE S. *The Meaning of Marriage.* Notre Dame Indiana: Fides Publishers Association, 1962 (Paperback).

HAGMAIER, GEORGE, C.S.P., AND GLEASON, ROBERT W., S.J. *Counselling the Catholic.* New York: Sheed and Ward, 1959.

HALEY, JOSEPH E., C.S.C. *Accent on Purity.* Notre Dame, Indiana: Fides Publishers, 1948 (Paperback).

HETTLINGER, RICHARD F. *Living With Sex: The Student's Dilemma.* New York: The Seabury Press, 1966.

IMBIORSKI, WALTER J. *Beginning Your Marriage.* Chicago, Illinois: Delaney Publications, 1966 (Paperback).

KENNEDY, JOHN F. *Profiles in Courage.* Memorial edition with a special foreword by Robert F. Kennedy. New York: Harper and Row, Publishers, 1964 (Perennial Library Paperback).

LEPP, IGNACE. *The Psychology of Loving.* Translated by Bernard B. Gilligan. New York: The New American Library, 1963 (Mentor-Omega Paperback). Published originally by Helicon Press, Inc., Baltimore, Maryland.

MARSHALL, JOHN, M.D. *Preparing For Marriage.* Baltimore, Maryland: Helicon Press, 1962 (Paperback).

MARRIAGE IS HOLY. Edited by H. Caffarel. Translated by Bernard G. Murchland, C.S.C. Notre Dame, Indiana: Fides Publishers, Inc., 1957 (Dome Paperback).

MASTERS, WILLIAM M. AND JOHNSON, VIRGINIA E. *Human Sexual Response.* Boston: Little, Brown and Co., 1966.

McCORMICK, RICHARD A., S.J. "The Priest and Teen-Age Sexuality." *All Things To All Men.* Edited by Joseph F. X. Cevetello. New York: Joseph F. Wagner, Inc., 1965.

MONDEN, LOUIS, S.J. *Sin, Liberty and Law.* Translated by Joseph Donceel, S.J. New York: Sheed and Ward, 1965.

ORAISON, MARC, M.D. *Learning To Love.* New York: Hawthorn Books, Inc., 1965.

PEALE, NORMAN VINCENT. *Sin, Sex and Self-Control.* Garden City, New York: Doubleday and Co., Inc., 1965.

SCHNACKENBURG, RUDOLF. *The Moral Teaching of the New Testament.* Translated by J. Holland-Smith and W. J. O'Hara. New York: Herder and Herder, 1966.

SCHULZ, CHARLES M. *Love Is Walking Hand In Hand.* San Francisco: Determined Productions, Inc., 1965.

Sex and the College Student. By the Committee on the College Student, Group for the Advancement of Psychiatry. New York: Fawcett World Library, 1966 (Paperback). Original hard-cover edition by Atheneum Publishers.

SHEDD, CHARLIE W. *Letters to Karen.* Nashville, Tennessee: Abingdon Press, 1965.

STAFFORD, EDWARD V., O.S.A. *Preparing for Marriage.* Chicago: Mentzer, Bush and Co., 1960 (Paperback).

SUENENS, LEON JOSEPH CARDINAL. *Love and Control.* Translated by George J. Robinson. Westminster, Maryland, 1963 (Paperback).

THIELICKE, HELMUT. *The Ethics of Sex.* Translated by John W. Doberstein. New York: Harper and Row, Publishers, 1964.

WATKIN, AELRED. *The Enemies of Love.* Glen Rock, New Jersey: Paulist Press, 1962 (Paperback).

Your Pre-Marriage Library. Chicago, Illinois: Delaney Publications, 1964 (Paperback).